From the Mouth of God

From the Mouth of God

Trusting, Reading, and Applying the Bible

Sinclair B. Ferguson

THE BANNER OF TRUTH TRUST

THE BANNER OF TRUTH TRUST

3 Murrayfield Road, Edinburgh EH12 6EL, UK
P.O. Box 621, Carlisle, PA 17013, USA

▪

© Sinclair B. Ferguson
First published as *Handle with Care!* by Hodder and Stoughton, 1982
This revised and enlarged edition, 2014
Reprinted 2014
Reprinted 2015

ISBN:
Print: 978 1 84871 242 3
Kindle: 978 1 84871 243 0
EPUB: 978 1 84871 244 7

▪

Typeset in 11/13 pt Adobe Garamond Pro at
The Banner of Truth Trust, Edinburgh

Printed in the USA by
Versa Press, Inc.,
East Peoria, IL

Contents

Introduction   ix

Part One – Trusting the Bible

1. It Is Written   3
2. Getting It Together   21
3. Is This God's Word?   49

Part Two – Reading the Bible

4. Do-It-Yourself   59
5. Keys   71
6. Prose, Poetry, Wisdom, and Prophecy   85
7. Gospels, Epistles, and Visions   109
8. For Example   131

Part Three – Applying the Bible

9. What's the Use?   151
10. Seeds Need Soil   163
11. Speaking Practically   175

Appendices

Appendix A: John Murray on 'The Guidance of the Holy Spirit'   183
Appendix B: John Newton on 'Divine Guidance'   189
Appendix C: Bibliography for Further Reading   195
Appendix D: Bible Reading Plan   197

Introduction

FROM *the Mouth of God* is about trusting, reading, and applying the Bible. Its title is drawn from the *English Standard Version* translation of Jesus' words in Matthew 4:4, which in turn are a quotation from Deuteronomy 8:3.

My own first encounter with these precise words was not in the English Bible itself (earlier translations had a different rendering), but as a teenager reading *The Scots Confession*, composed in 1560 by the Scottish reformer John Knox and five companions, all memorably sharing the Christian name 'John'.

In their Preface to the *Confession* they gave a striking assurance to their readers:

> If any man will note in our Confession any chapter or sentence contrary to God's Holy Word, that it would please him of his gentleness and for Christian charity's sake to inform us of it in writing; and we, upon our honour, do promise him that by God's grace we shall give him satisfaction *from the mouth of God*, that is, from Holy Scripture, or else we shall alter whatever he can prove to be wrong.

Even although familiar with the words of Matthew 4:4 in the *Authorized Version* (King James) and the *Revised Standard Version*, I remember being struck by this bold description of the Bible. Somehow it seemed much more arresting than the vocabulary more commonly used in the New Testament ('Scripture', 'it is written', 'inspired by God'). In some respects it presented an even more vivid picture than the modern 'God-breathed'—and all the more so because this was the description our Saviour chose to use. This was how he viewed the Scriptures. They were the very mouth of his heavenly Father, and so 'every word' they contain must be important. It was them he had in view when he applied to himself the beautiful words of Isaiah's third 'Servant Song':

> The Lord GOD has given me
>   the tongue of those who are taught,
> that I may know how to sustain with a word
>   him who is weary.
> Morning by morning he awakens;
>   he awakens my ear
>   to hear as those who are taught.
> The Lord GOD has opened my ear,
>   and I was not rebellious.[1]

From the Mouth of God is essentially an expanded study of this powerful description of the Bible. It sets out to explore three questions:

First, why it is that Christians throughout the ages have believed, with Jesus, that the Bible is God's mouth, from which his word is heard.

Second, how should we approach reading the Bible in order to gain a better understanding and appreciation of its message?

Third, how can we do this in a way that is well-grounded in Scripture and that actually helps us get to know the message of the Bible better?

These pages do not have specialists in view, but ordinary Christians who want to think through what we should believe about the Bible, and how we can go about understanding and applying its life-transforming message.

Since it is not a technical or academic treatise it may be helpful to explain why it has so many footnotes! Most of them have been included to help readers locate the biblical basis for what is being said. Some readers will want to look them up, take them in, and reflect on their teaching. Others may simply want to note their presence and read on. If so they can do that comfortably by simply ignoring the superscript numbers. But I hope they will perhaps return again to certain sections for closer and deeper study.

---

[1] *Isa.* 50:4-5.

From the Mouth of God is a book with a pre-history. Some thirty plus years ago, I hurriedly wrote a little book on the Bible called *Handle with Care* which Hodder and Stoughton graciously published[1] in place of the book on the Trinity I had—in a moment of over-ambitious enthusiasm—contracted to write for them but failed to complete. Over the years I have had requests to reprint *Handle with Care*. But a book written half a lifetime ago, by a young man with a somewhat guilty conscience and in a hurry, needed re-read and re-written. Even had there been the desire to do that, other responsibilities demanded priority. But no one has been more persevering in asking for the book than Jonathan Watson, General Editor of The Banner of Truth and I am grateful now for his dogged encouragement to, and patience with, a procrastinating author!

The conviction that lay behind writing about the Bible in the first place was that God's word is itself the worker in the life of the individual Christian and in the fellowship and outreach of the church. In the intervening decades this conviction has only been strengthened through the privileges of seminary teaching, preaching and pastoring. I am deeply grateful for the privilege of witnessing the transforming impact of Scripture on so many men and women, students and children as God's word has done its own work.

The dedication of these pages is an expression of gratitude for four decades and more of friendship with Ian and Joan Hamilton, and marks the fifteenth anniversary of their ministry in Cambridge Presbyterian Church.

My deepest human debt, as always, is to those who know me best, and have loved me most, my wife Dorothy and our family, who provide the context that makes possible the solitary discipline of writing. And beyond that, my great debt beyond payment, is to the God who has spoken in his word, and has made himself known to us as a loving Father, a gracious Saviour, and an indwelling Spirit.

SINCLAIR B. FERGUSON
June 2014

---

[1] First published by Hodder and Stoughton in 1982.

Part One – Trusting the Bible

1. It Is Written

THE words 'it is written', or a similar phrase, appear around ninety times in the New Testament. These three words[1] settled matters for Jesus and the apostles. If Scripture said it, then God said it.[2] They regarded the Bible as God's own word. Through it he speaks.[3] To it Christians listen. Its teaching Christians believe. Its commands Christians obey. Its pages Christians love.

Christianity has always been a Bible-based religion. Our beliefs, lifestyle, and day-to-day experience as Christians are profoundly shaped by this composite volume of sixty-six books, containing some sixteen hundred pages of closely printed information. Yet we are so used to the existence of what we call 'The Bible' that we rarely ask: Why do we have a Bible at all?

It is, after all, only in the last four hundred years or so that ordinary people have owned their own copies of the Bible. Only the combination of the invention of the printing press and the events of the sixteenth-century Reformation eventually brought it into every Christian home. Thus, for the longer part of the history of the Christian church, daily Bible-reading was the luxury of the few rather than the privilege of the many.

[1] Only one word in Greek (*gegraptai*).

[2] A point underlined in great detail and at length by B. B. Warfield in: "'It Says:' "Scripture Says:" "God Says"' originally written in 1899 and republished in the influential first volume of his collected works, *Revelation and Inspiration* (New York: Oxford University Press, 1932), pp. 281-332.

[3] The point powerfully illustrated by the way in which *Heb.* 12:5 introduces a quotation from *Prov.* 3:11-12 with the words 'And have you forgotten the exhortation that addresses you as sons.' Notice the *present* tense ('addresses') and the second person plural pronoun ('you').

Why the Bible?

The brief answer is that Christians believe God communicates through the Bible. He reveals himself in its pages, speaks in its sentences and does so in order to bring us to trust, know, and love him. Through the Bible God makes himself known to us, just as we make our thoughts and plans known to others through the words we speak. To change the metaphor, it acts as the lens through which we begin to see who he is, what he has done for us, and what his will is for our lives. As a result we come to know him for ourselves and to know ourselves better.

This is what the Bible is for. If it does not achieve this goal, then the failure cannot be laid at its door. It is we who have not yet begun to use it properly.

Yet there is more to the Bible than this. God's word comes to us in our spiritual sickness and blindness. We are ill spiritually—indeed fatally so—according to Scripture. By nature we are spiritually blind and dead.[1] Scripture therefore provides God's eyesight-restoring and life-giving prescription for our spiritual sickness.

Paul explains our need:

> Men ... by their unrighteousness suppress the truth. For what can be known about God is plain to them, because God has shown it to them. For his invisible attributes, namely, his eternal power and divine nature, have been clearly perceived, ever since the creation of the world, in the things that have been made. So they are without excuse. For although they knew God, they did not honour him as God or give thanks to him, but they became futile in their thinking, and their foolish hearts were darkened. Claiming to be wise, they became fools, and exchanged the glory of the immortal God for images resembling mortal man and birds and animals and reptiles.[2]

God made man as his image (*Gen.* 1:26-27), in important respects like him, and capable of receiving communication from him and experiencing communion with him. We were made to know and to enjoy our Creator.

---

[1] See *Eph.* 2:1, 5.
[2] *Rom.* 1:18-23.

God also expressed his character in everything he made. He painted into the created order expressions of his being, his kindness, and indeed all the facets of his deity, 'his eternal power and divine nature'.

Sometimes when we watch a magnificent sunset, or look up at the vastness of a star-and-planet decorated night sky, or look down on a newborn sleeping baby, we feel our breath almost taken away with a sense of wonder. That is surely just a taste of what it must have been like to see with perfect vision the way God's hand shaped creation and to experience both adoration and joy in his presence.

Furthermore our first parents were created with a sense that they had been made by a loving God (they were made as his image and likeness). So they were not only surrounded by a world that expressed his character, but also invaded by a deep consciousness that they were made by him and for him. As Abraham Kuyper put it (echoing John Calvin's idea that the creation is a theatre of God's glory[1]): 'If the cosmos is the theatre of revelation, in this theatre man is both actor and spectator.'[2]

But now woven into these moments of awe is also a homesickness for a lost past.

Genesis 3 tells us the sad story of how the first man and woman, made as God's image, created to enjoy fellowship with him, doubted his goodness, rejected his wisdom, rebelled against his authority, and were therefore banished from his presence.

Yet God's revelation of himself persists (note the present tenses in what follows):

> The heavens declare the glory of God,
>   and the sky above proclaims his handiwork.
> Day to day pours out speech,
>   and night to night reveals knowledge.
> There is no speech, nor are there words,
>   whose voice is not heard.
> Their measuring line goes out through all the earth,
>   and their words to the end of the world.[3]

[1] John Calvin, *Institutes of the Christian Religion*, tr. F. L. Battles; ed. J. T. McNeill, (Philadelphia, Westminster Press, 1960), I.vi.2; I.xiv.20 and elsewhere.

[2] Abraham Kuyper, *Encyclopaedia of Sacred Theology*, tr. J. H. de Vries (New York: Funk & Wagnalls, 1900), p. 264.

[3] *Psa.* 19:1-4.

There is no 'where' to which we can go in order to escape from God's self revelation, or from the innate sense we have that he is God.

All this may still be true (and is, according to the Bible's testimony), but it is certainly not how people see things. Many question the goodness of God. Some angrily repudiate his very existence. They claim to see no evidence of his presence, and deny that there are any substantial reasons for belief that this world is a creation. In this respect, 'All around is in darkness' they say. 'There is no light in the universe which leads us to God' is their claim.

These reactions come as no surprise to Christians. Our Bibles have already provided an analysis of them.

But the Christian knows that the facts of the matter are very different. The darkness is not *outside*, but *inside*. We have become futile in our thinking, and our hearts have become darkened. God's wonderful power, and his nature as the living, loving God, can still be seen in everything which he has made. Even the marred creation still bears the marks of the Creator's loving hand. We are the ones who are blind.

This is the tragedy of the human condition. Creation sings its hymns of praise to God every day even while the melancholy strains of its fallen condition are heard. And through it all the Divine Composer continues to conduct his symphony of love for the world. We 'know God', says Paul, since we continue to be invaded (because we are his image) and surrounded (in creation) by his revelation. But we do not count this knowledge worth having. We suppress and repress its impact on our minds, wills and emotions. As a result we do not, indeed cannot by nature, know God as our God or trust him as our loving Heavenly Father.[1]

John Calvin sums this up well:

> It is therefore in vain that so many burning lamps shine for us in the workmanship of the universe to show forth the glory of its Author. Although they bathe us wholly in their radiance, yet they can of themselves in no way lead us into the right path. Surely they strike some sparks, but before their fuller light shines forth, these are smothered. For this reason, the apostle ... means ... that the invisible divinity is made manifest in such spectacles, but that we have not the

[1] See *Rom.* 1:18-25.

eyes to see this unless they be illumined by the inner revelation of God through faith.[1]

The story line of the Bible is therefore as follows:

Despite this rejection and rebellion, the Creator has been extraordinarily gracious. Seeing us in our inability to know and love him, to understand and serve him, he has come to redeem and restore us.

God has done this by a series of mighty acts throughout history, culminating in the coming of Christ, whom he sent to bring us back into fellowship with himself. In addition he has given his own explanation and interpretation of his actions in his word.

The author of Hebrews summarises this centuries-long process in these words:

> Long ago, at many times and in many ways, God spoke to our fathers by the prophets, but in these last days he has spoken to us by his Son, whom he appointed the heir of all things, through whom also he created the world.[2]

Notice here several important features of God's self-revelation:

First, it is *historical*: God has been active in history in order to show his power and love.

Second, it is *verbal*: God has provided his own interpretation of his actions. He has given us a permanent record of his words and the significance of his deeds through those who wrote the pages of Scripture.

Third, it is *progressive and cumulative*: God gave his revelation in different ways and at different times. But now he has given his final revelation in 'these last days'.

Fourth, it is *Christ-centred*: God's revelation reached its fulfilment when he spoke his final word to us in his Son, Jesus Christ.

God has thus revealed himself in act, word, and person. Scripture is the record of this revelation. It is, as a whole, the book of 'the revelation of Jesus Christ which God gave ... .'[3] Its purpose, as Paul succinctly puts it is 'to make you wise for salvation through faith in Christ Jesus'.[4] From Genesis 3 to Revelation 22 the Bible is about salvation.

[1] John Calvin, *The Institutes of the Christian Religion*, I.v.14.
[2] *Heb.* 1:1-2.
[3] These opening words of the last book in the Bible (*Rev.* 1:1) are thus applicable to the whole Bible.
[4] *2 Tim.* 3;15.

The necessity of Scripture

It would in theory be possible to know about God's revelation even if there had never been a Bible. The story could have been passed on from one generation to the next. In an oral culture where memorization was highly developed that in fact is what happened.

But think of those party games in which a message is whispered from one person to another around the room, and ends up distorted sometimes almost beyond recognition. How different it would be if the original message had been written down on paper and then passed round the room!

God is committed to preserving the message of his saving grace. He knows that our memories are short, our tongues as well as our hearts are deceitful. For this reason he has given us a written record and interpretation of his saving activity. The Bible thus preserves for us, in reliable form, what could have become garbled and distorted over the succeeding centuries. In addition its message can now readily be made known in every place and time. Herman Bavinck puts this well:

> The written word ... does not die upon the air but lives on; it is not, like oral traditions, subject to falsification; ... it is not limited in scope to the few people who hear it, but is the kind of thing, rather, which can spread out to all peoples and to all lands. Writing makes permanent the spoken word, protects it against falsification, and disseminates it far and wide.[1]

Personal communication

The Bible was not meant primarily for scholars or as a text-book for schools and colleges. It is, rather, God's personal communication to us. It has a life-restoring-and-transforming goal in view: to bring light to our darkened minds and faith to our dead hearts. Scripture thus makes a profound impact on us as we read it or hear it as the word of God. Through it God tells us how much he loves us,[2] and how we

---

[1] H. Bavinck, *Our Reasonable Faith*, translated from the Dutch by Henry Zylstra (Grand Rapids: Baker Book House, 1956), p. 96.

[2] Christians can sing 'Jesus loves me this I know' because they can add '*For the Bible tells me so*'. It is almost universally acknowledged among theists, Unitarians and others that God is love. But if one rejects the Scriptures of the Old and New Testaments as a divine revelation, and is thus forced to ground one's conviction of

can know and serve him. That is why it is important for us to be sure that what we are reading really is a message from God.

Once we know this, we have all the incentive we need to work hard to understand Scripture. We will take whatever steps are necessary to become better acquainted with the mind and will of God in the Bible.

The Bible presents itself to us as both a divine and a human book. It is God's word. Yet it was written by men. It is the word of God in the mouths of men.[1]

How this happens is what we call the *inspiration* of Scripture.

Inspiration

The term ' inspiration' is drawn from the older English translations of 2 Timothy 3:16. For example the Geneva Bible of 1560 rendered Paul's words: 'The whole Scripture is given by inspiration of God'.

But what do we mean when we say that the Bible is 'inspired by God'? We do not mean that every sentence in it is *inspiring*. Many are; but some are also very mundane.

Sometimes the apparently mundane turns out to be wonderfully inspiring. The opening section of the Gospel of Matthew is an example. Read simply as a list of names it leaves most of us bored. Read as it is meant to be, as the story of God's plan unfolding from the time of Abraham until the coming of Christ, and it turns out to be a thrilling survey of God's sovereign Lordship over history.

But 'inspiration' does not mean the Bible is inspiring like a beautiful and moving symphony or a deeply poignant poem. In fact when Paul wrote that all Scripture is 'inspired by God',[2] he was not thinking about its *effect on us* (inspiring),[3] but about its *source in him*.

God as love on phenomena, the signals seem to be mixed. There can be no satisfactory theodicy without the revelation of the Scriptures with their centre on the coming of God the Son into his fractured world to redeem and restore it. The Christian's conviction that God is love is anchored in the way he demonstrated that love in Christ on the cross in his death for our sins and in the way his resurrection inaugurates a new world, *Rom.* 5:8; 8:32.

[1] See *Jer.* 1:9; 5:14 for this concept. Cf. also *2 Sam.* 23:2; *Isa.* 59:21; *Acts* 1:16; 3:21; *Heb.* 1:1.

[2] *2 Tim.* 3: 16 Authorised (King James) Version—the only text in which, strictly speaking, the Scriptures are described as 'inspired'.

[3] He describes its effect or usefulness *later* in the verse when he explains the way in which Scripture is 'profitable' or useful in our lives.

B. B. Warfield explains:

> It is very desirable that we should free ourselves at the outset from influences arising from the current employment of the term 'inspiration' ... This term is not a Biblical term, and its etymological implications[1] are not perfectly accordant with the Biblical conception of the modes of the Divine operation in giving the Scriptures. The Biblical writers do not conceive of the Scriptures as a human product breathed into by the Divine Spirit, and thus heightened in its qualities or endowed with new qualities; but as a Divine product produced through the instrumentality of men. They do not conceive of these men, by whose instrumentality Scripture is produced, as working upon their own initiative, though energized by God to greater effort and higher achievement, but as moved by the Divine initiative and borne by the irresistible power of the Spirit of God along ways of His choosing to ends of His appointment.[2]

It might seem odd that one of the most persuasive defenders of the authority of the Bible should have had reservations about the term 'inspiration'. But what Warfield meant is that Scripture is not an object *into which* God breathed, but something which God himself has 'breathed out'. For this reason modern Bible translations of 2 Timothy 3:16 render Paul's word *theopneustos* as 'breathed out by God'[3] or as 'God-breathed'.[4]

The inspiration of Scripture, therefore, is not a matter of God *breathing into* ('in-spire')[5] what men had already written. It involves God *breathing* out his word('ex-spire'). He is the origin, the source, of what men wrote. This is why there are several places in the New Testament where the expressions, 'God said' and 'Scripture said' seem to be interchangeable. If Scripture has said it, then (since Scripture is God-breathed) we can say, God has said it.[6]

---

[1] The root meaning, history and significance of the word itself.

[2] In his article 'Inspiration' in *Revelation and Inspiration*, p. 99.

[3] ESV.

[4] NIV.

[5] From the Latin verb *spiro* to breathe and the preposition *in* meaning in or into.

[6] See *Gal.* 3:8; *Rom.* 9:17 where 'Scripture' is really the equivalent of 'God'; and *Matt.* 19:4, 5 (quoting *Gen.* 2:24); *Heb.* 3:7 (quoting *Psa.* 95:7); *Acts* 4:24, 25 (quoting

But how does this take place?

Concurrence

Undoubtedly the human writers of Scripture were conscious that they were expressing their own thoughts as they wrote. But at the same time they were under the sovereign direction of the Spirit. Theologians call this two-dimensional reality 'concurrence'.[1]

God works in his ordinary providence in a way that involves concurrence. He is active in bringing about his purposes, yet at the same time we are also active in a significant way. In one and the same event God is active in a 'God way' while we are active in a 'human way'.[2] We cannot collapse these two dimensions into one and apportion, say, fifty per cent of the action to God and fifty per cent to man.

There is mystery here, of course, since God is God and we are not. But the concept of concurrence prevents us from adopting a mistaken logic and concluding that if God is active in an event then to that extent man must be inactive.

Classic illustrations of this biblical principle are found in the stories of Joseph and Daniel:

Human action:	As for you, you meant evil against me,
Divine action:	but God meant it for good.

Human action:	In the third year of the reign of Jehoiakim king of Judah, Nebuchadnezzar king of Babylon came to Jerusalem and besieged it.
Divine action:	And the Lord gave Jehoiakim king of Judah into his hand.[3]

Psa. 2:1) where what 'Scripture says' is regarded as equivalent to what 'God says'.

[1] The Latin term is *concursus* (from the verb *concurro*, the root of our English word 'concurrent') denoting two or more agents acting together in one and the same event.

[2] Since he is the infinite Creator and we are finite creatures, he inevitably relates to space-time reality in a way that is different from the way we do.

[3] *Gen.* 50:20; *Dan.* 1:1-2.

Peter's sermon on the Day of Pentecost also provides an illustration:

Divine action:	This Jesus, delivered up according to the definite plan and foreknowledge of God,
Human action:	you crucified and killed by the hands of lawless men.

Rather than say 'God was fifty per cent responsible while men accomplished the other fifty per cent', Scripture teaches us that both God and man were fully active. This is concurrence.

The inspiration of the Bible is a special example of concurrence. God fulfils his purpose by means of secondary causation.[1] God was one hundred per cent engaged in *breathing out* his word; the human authors were one hundred per cent active in *writing out* that word. The first Christians clearly understood this. Thus, for example, when they quoted from Psalm 2:1-2 they interpreted these words to entail God speaking by the Holy Spirit through the mouth of King David.[2]

Peter comments that the authors of Scripture were 'carried along by the Holy Spirit' whom he identifies as 'the Spirit of Christ in them'. He thus indicates (a) that both the Old and New Testaments are the fruit of the activity of the same Spirit of Christ; (b) that the Spirit not only shaped the author's lives providentially but worked actively in them as they were writing. All they wrote was what the Spirit intended to communicate. Thus the 'inspiration' of Scripture, like the apostles' ability to work miracles, is a special example of the concursive activity of God.

This concursive activity—God giving his word but doing so through human instruments—was a major element in the ministry of the apostles. There were, therefore, two elements involved in the inspiration of the Scriptures. God (i) over-ruled the lives of those who wrote the Bible in ways that would prepare them to write it, and in addition he (ii) superintended their lives as they wrote.

[1] *2 Pet.* 1:21 (the verb conveys the sense of being brought to an intended destination); *1 Pet.* 1:11. *The Westminster Confession of Faith,* (V.2) well expresses the idea: 'Although, in relation to the decree of God, the first Cause, all things come to pass immutably, and infallibly; yet, by the same providence, He ordereth them to fall out, according to the nature of second causes, either necessarily, freely, or contingently.' (repr. Glasgow: Free Presbyterian Publications, 1976).

[2] *Acts* 4:24-26.

Same Spirit, a variety of ways of working

B. B. Warfield pointedly describes the superintending work of God in preparing the authors of Scripture:

> If God wished to give His people a series of letters like Paul's, he prepared a Paul to write them, and the Paul He brought to the task was a Paul who spontaneously would write just such letters.[1]

When Warfield first expressed that view, he was suspected by some Christians of denying the inspiration of the Bible! But that suspicion was rooted in the (false) idea that if the Bible is divinely inspired it cannot have come to us in such an apparently mundane way. The writers could not have had any substantial role in its writing. At root, however, this *presupposes* a view of biblical inspiration instead of listening to what the text of Scripture itself says about its origins.

The Bible is a composite work, written by various men at different times. Their writings all bear the stamp of their different personalities, backgrounds, concerns and gifts. Isaiah had a different temperament from Jeremiah. It is virtually impossible to imagine either of them writing Ezekiel. Peter was differently wired from John—and it shows in their writings.

Furthermore, the books of the Bible were composed in very different ways. Very few parts of it came in the context of unusual mystical experiences.

Again, the book of Psalms slowly developed over an extended period of time. It reflects, perhaps more than any other Old Testament book, the full spectrum of ordinary human experience and emotions. But under God's loving superintendence the authors were being given words by which to express every aspect of human experience. Here, what 'David wrote' is what 'God breathed'.[2]

Or take the 'God-breathed' Scripture we know as Luke's Gospel. How was it given to the church? The author tells us:

> It seemed good to me also, having followed all things closely for some time past, to write an orderly account for you, most

[1] Warfield, *op. cit.*, p. 101.
[2] *Matt.* 22:43; *Mark* 12:56; *Acts* 1:16; 4:25; *Heb.* 4:7.

excellent Theophilus, that you may have certainty concerning the things you have been taught.[1]

Historical research lies behind Luke's Gospel. The Spirit shaped him with gifts and opportunities to do this and also superintended his activity.

To give another example, no book in the New Testament is more 'supernatural' than Revelation. It is, after all, *revelation* given by Jesus himself.[2]

Yet in it John frequently describes what *he saw*.[3] It is clear that the lenses through which he 'saw' were crafted according to a prescription filled with Old Testament imagery and language. He did not make up the vision.[4] Rather—to apply Warfield's principle that if God wanted the book of Revelation he prepared a John to write it—the aged seer's mind had so absorbed the Old Testament that he recognized the imagery he saw and described it in terms of its Old Testament connections. The Revelation which comes from Christ is given to us through a fully human author. *So* the Bible presents itself as both a divine and a human book from start to finish.

Thus, if we want to know *how* any section of Scripture came as 'God-breathed' we need to listen to the clues it gives us about the way in which it was actually written.

The great chain (of revelation)

Jesus gave some of his profoundest teaching to his disciples on the night of his betrayal. He spoke of leaving them, but assured them he would send the Spirit in his place:

> But the Helper, the Holy Spirit, whom the Father will send in my name, he will teach you all things and bring to your remembrance all that I have said to you.[5]

[1] *Luke* 1:3-4.
[2] *Rev.* 1:1-2.
[3] For example, *Rev.* 1:12; 5:1; 6:9; 7:1, *etc.*
[4] Sometimes commentators seem to fall into the trap of tracing the biblical allusions in Revelation as though John had consciously pieced the vision together himself from the Old Testament.
[5] *John* 14:26.

When the Spirit of truth comes, he will guide you into all the truth, for he will not speak on his own authority, but whatever he hears he will speak, and he will declare to you the things that are to come.[1]

Here are three promises. The apostles would (1) remember the words of Christ, (2) understand the truth (of Christ), and (3) see the future fulfilment of his kingdom. Where, if anywhere, do we find the fulfilment of these promises? The answer is surely: 'In the pages of the New Testament'.

This becomes even clearer in John 17 when Jesus prays for the apostles and for all who would later come to faith:

- *He received the words he spoke from his Father.* His words were his Father's words. It was as if the Father had made him his 'power of attorney' to speak on his behalf and with his authority.

- *He then gave these words to the apostles.* They had received and believed them. Now, in turn, he made them his 'power of attorney'.

- *The apostles' task was now to give those words to others* who would come to believe in Jesus.[2]

Here (in words spoken exclusively to those in the Upper Room), Jesus was preparing his apostles to give the New Testament to the church![3] This was what he had in view when he promised that the Spirit would remind them of his words, lead them into the truth, and reveal the things that were still to come.

Their 'word' thus became the contents of the New Testament: Gospels (what Jesus said); Epistles (the truth about Jesus); and the Prophecies (including Revelation—the things still to come). In these ways—memory of things said, understanding of the gospel, a sense

[1] *John* 16:13.

[2] See *John* 17: 7, 8, 14, 20.

[3] It is worth noting here in passing, by way of *caveat*, that many Christians have a tendency to apply Jesus' words in *John* 14:26 and 16:13 (especially the latter, '[The Spirit] will guide you into all the truth') directly to themselves. But we were not present in the Upper Room. These words were not directed to us. Their fulfillment is found in the ministry of the apostles. If they have any application to us it surely involves our searching the Scriptures where the apostles recorded the truth into which the Spirit led them.

of future things—God would 'breathe out' through them the New Testament Scriptures to add to the Old Testament which they already believed was God's word on the authority of their Master.

The apostle Paul traces a parallel chain of revelation when he speaks about his own ministry in the context of his discussion of the wisdom of the world and the wisdom of God.[1] He had not used the style of the classical orators ('lofty speech or wisdom') but the rhetoric of the cross. Nor was his disposition one of a self-assurance based on his talents and training, but of 'weakness ... fear and much trembling'. Yet his speech and message were 'in demonstration of the Spirit and of power, that your faith might not rest in the wisdom of men but in the power of God'.[2]

Here Paul gives expression to the principle of concursive operation in his ministry: 'my speech and my message ... in demonstration of the Spirit'.[3] This is further indicated when he teaches the churches: the wisdom of God has been 'revealed to us through the Spirit'. Indeed God had given him the Spirit so that he 'might understand the things freely given us by God'.

There is a further dimension here to the 'chain of revelation'. The Father gave the Son his words; he in turn had given the words to the apostles; they were to speak these words with the authority of the Father and the Son. This they would be enabled to do when the Father and the Son sent the Spirit to them.

The Spirit has now come with full power of attorney since he 'searches everything, even the depths of God'.[4] Paul has been commissioned into this 'chain of revelation' for the wisdom of God 'has been revealed to [him] through the Spirit'.[5] Now he can impart it to others 'in words ... taught by the Spirit'.[6] His experience is parallel to that of the prophets: God places 'my words in your mouth'—the simplest expression of concursive operation. And like the prophets of

---

[1] *1 Cor.* 1: 18-2:16.
[2] *1 Cor.* 2:3-4.
[3] *1 Cor.* 2:4.
[4] *1 Cor.* 2:10.
[5] *1 Cor.* 2:10.
[6] *1 Cor.* 2:13. Note Paul's significant reference here to 'in words' (*logois*).

the old covenant, Paul as a minister of the new covenant[1] is conscious that this divine activity extends even to the words that he uses.

Recognising the divine origin and inspiration of apostolic Scripture is essential if we are to adopt a right attitude to it. Like the Thessalonians we need to have 'received the word of God ... [and] accepted it not as the word of men [merely] but as what it really is, the word of God, which is at work in you believers'.[2]

In revealing himself to us God expresses his infinite, beginningless, triune being to our created and finite capacities. When he communicates to us he does so in a medium that is consistent with his own being, yet at the same time calibrated to our modes of communication and levels of understanding. Necessarily so. This is often referred to as the principle of *divine accommodation*. It applies not only to the general revelation of creation but also to the special revelation given in Scripture.

Accommodation

It is well known now that the New Testament was not written in classical Greek, or a specially sanctified form of the language, but rather in *koinē* (common) Greek—the language of the people. God meets us where we are, and comes down to our level to be understood. The Bible is not given to us in the tongues of angels but of men. God has condescended to speak to his rebellious creatures in a language used in the ordinary course of life.

John Calvin famously expressed this principle when he wrote:

> Who even of slight intelligence does not understand that, as nurses commonly do with infants, God is wont in a measure to 'lisp' in speaking to us? Thus such forms of speaking do not so much express clearly what God is like as accommodate the knowledge of him to our slight capacity. To do this he must descend far beneath his loftiness.[3]

In saying this he was simply echoing Augustine:

> ... go on making progress by walking more slowly with scripture at your side, where she does not desert your

[1] *2 Cor.* 3:6.
[2] *1 Thess.* 2:13.
[3] Calvin, *Institutes*, I.xiii.1.

weakness but matches her steps to yours in motherly fashion. For she speaks, you see, in such a way that she mocks the proud by her sublimity, fills the attentive with awe at her profundity, feeds the mature with her truthfulness, fosters the little ones with her kindliness.[1]

To such a condescending God of grace we do well to listen carefully!

Reading the Bible

All of this has immediate implications for the way we read and study the Bible.

For example, if we understand that God has spoken through human penmen, in human language, it should prevent us falling into the trap of looking for hidden meanings in a passage.

Instead our approach will be to read passages in the light of the historical context and circumstances of the author. We will try to discover what was in the mind of the writer when he wrote, what he was saying to his contemporaries, and in that context we will ask how all this fits into the overall teaching of Scripture. In this context we may safely ask questions like 'What does this passage say/mean, and how does it apply to me/us today?' But if instead we look for special meanings lying hidden underneath the text, we will end up applying God's word in ways quite different from those he intends.[2]

The Bible did not fall directly from heaven. Every word that proceeded from the mouth of God has come to us through the instrumentality of men and finds its place within the bigger story of God's redemptive purposes.

Paul's letter to the Romans, for example, should not be read as though it teaches 'eternal truths' unrelated to specific 'temporal events'. It was (i) dictated by Paul; (ii) written by Tertius;[3] (iii) carried

---

[1] *On Genesis in the Literal Sense*, trs. E. Hill and J. E. Rotelle (New York: New City Press, 2002), p. 279.

[2] If it is asked, 'How then have such interpretations helped and guided people?', the answer is that often what is wrongly derived from a passage may nevertheless be a biblical truth. But this means only that our general knowledge of Scripture has preserved us from a principle of interpretation that may actually lead to disaster.

[3] *Rom.* 16:22.

to Rome, probably by Phoebe,[1] and (iv) was read out to the church there. It had an autobiographical context in Paul's life, a specific message for the churches in Rome, and also some pastoral teaching relevant to their current church life. Paul wrote that he longed to see and serve these Roman Christians.[2] He was also keen that they would be willing to become, like the church at Antioch, a 'sending church' for him as he embarked on a new mission to Spain.[3] It is within the context of these and other elements in the story line into which Romans fits that we are able to apply the letter's teaching to our own setting, even while we are reading about its application to its original setting.

God has spoken. Amazingly he has come down to our level, like a father talking to his children. He has humbled himself by using frail mortals to communicate his infallible word. Realizing this, when we open the pages of Scripture we will humbly bow before the Lord of Scripture and pray that through it we will hear him as the gracious speaking God he is. Samuel's prayer can hardly be improved upon: 'Speak, Lord, for your servant hears.'[4]

---

[1] *Rom.* 16:1-2.
[2] *Rom.* 1:11.
[3] *Rom.* 15:24.
[4] *1 Sam.* 3:10.

2. Getting It Together

WE began the first chapter by asking the fundamental question: Why do we have a Bible at all?

But there is a second basic question which we now need to ask. How did the Bible—these sixty-six books written over many centuries—come to be bound together in one volume?

Children in Sunday School used to be given a little card with a picture of a book-case divided into several sections, holding all the books of the Bible. The sections were headed: 'History', 'Prophecy', 'Gospels', 'Letters', and so on. It was meant as an encouragement to memorize the books of the Bible. It also taught them that the Bible is not one single book, but a collection of different kinds of books composed over many centuries.

We take it for granted that this is our Bible.

But how do we know which books should be in the library? How did they get there in the first place? How can we be sure we have the right books? Can we add more books to the Bible? And, anyway, what practical difference does it make?

Canon

Anglicanism's *Thirty-nine Articles*[1] and Presbyterianism's *Westminster Confession of Faith*[2] both list sixty-six books as the word of God. This is the 'canon' of Scripture for the Christian.

---

[1] The traditional foundational doctrinal confession of the Church of England and Episcopalians world wide.

[2] The traditional foundational doctrinal confession of Presbyterians world wide.

'Canon' is a Greek word (*kanōn*). It originally meant a reed, or a straight rod.[1] Since rods were employed for measuring things it came to be used as the word for a standard of measurement, and so for a rule to guide and govern action. It is used in the New Testament in this sense:[2] 'And as for all who walk by this *rule,* peace and mercy be upon them, and upon the Israel of God.'[3] The 'rule' (*kanōn*) in view is the new creation in Christ. Paul's point in this context is that the principle of acceptance with God and fellowship among his people is new life in Christ, not whether a person has been circumcised or not.

During the early centuries of the Christian Church the term 'canon' described first the 'rule of faith' which believers confessed. It then became the term of choice to describe the New Testament as the 'rule of faith and life' by which the whole church was governed.

But how did this development take place?

The Old Testament canon

Moses wrote down in permanent form the revelation which was given to him by God:

> Moses came and told the people all the words of the LORD and all the rules. And all the people answered with one voice and said, 'All the words that the LORD has spoken we will do.' And Moses wrote down all the words of the LORD. He rose early in the morning and built an altar at the foot of the mountain, and twelve pillars, according to the twelve tribes of Israel. And he sent young men of the people of Israel, who offered burnt offerings and sacrificed peace offerings of oxen to the LORD. And Moses took half of the blood and put it in basins, and half of the blood he threw against the altar. Then he took the Book of the Covenant and read it in the hearing of the people. And they said, 'All that the LORD has spoken we will do, and we will be obedient.' And Moses

---

[1] Alexander Souter comments interestingly, 'Besides being straight, it had to be incapable of bending'. A. Souter, *The Text and Canon of the New Testament*, revised by C. S. C. Williams (London, Duckworth & Co., 1913), second edition 1954, p. 141.

[2] For example in *2 Cor.* 10:13, 15, 16.

[3] *Gal.* 6:16.

took the blood and threw it on the people and said, 'Behold the blood of the covenant that the Lord has made with you in accordance with all these words.'[1]

Deuteronomy later records the closing days of Moses' life. It describes the arrangements he made for the future of God's people. He spoke to Joshua at a great public gathering, ordained him into his new role as leader of God's people, and assured him of the help of God. But he made a further provision:

Then Moses wrote this law and gave it to the priests, the sons of Levi, who carried the ark of the covenant of the Lord, and to all the elders of Israel. And Moses commanded them, 'At the end of every seven years, at the set time in the year of release, at the Feast of Booths, when all Israel comes to appear before the Lord your God at the place that he will choose, you shall read this law before all Israel in their hearing. Assemble the people, men, women, and little ones, and the sojourner within your towns, that they may hear and learn to fear the Lord your God, and be careful to do all the words of this law, and that their children, who have not known it, may hear and learn to fear the Lord your God, as long as you live in the land that you are going over the Jordan to possess.'[2]

God appointed a new leader. But he also gave the people a written canon, and made it clear that the latter always exercised authority over the former. This is further underlined in his exhortation to Joshua at the beginning of his ministry as Moses' successor:

Only be strong and very courageous, being careful to do according to all the law that Moses my servant commanded you. Do not turn from it to the right hand or to the left, that you may have good success wherever you go. This Book of the Law shall not depart from your mouth, but you shall meditate on it day and night, so that you may be careful to do according to all that is written in it. For then you will make your way prosperous, and then you will have good success. Have I not commanded you? Be strong and courageous. Do not be

---

[1] *Exod.* 24:3-8.
[2] *Deut.* 31:9-13.

frightened, and do not be dismayed, for the LORD your God is with you wherever you go." [1]

The Book of the Covenant, the word of God, in its written form—Scripture—became the rule, the canon, by which Joshua and all the people of God were to govern their lives. It was to be their 'Bible'. [2] As they responded in faith and obedience they lived in God's blessing. If they rebelled in unbelief and disobedience they placed their lives outside of the sphere of covenant blessing and were exposed to God's judgment curse. The immense authority of God's written word was therefore symbolised by the fact that it was to be placed beside the Ark of the Covenant. Together they represented the Presence of God among his people (Ark) and the Pleasure of God for his people (Book). [3]

The Old Testament as a whole contains the story of how God's people were shaped by their faithfulness, or faithlessness, to this covenant word. Their history is interpreted by this principle; all worship is a reflection of it; in a sense all prophecy is an application and enlargement of it.

We see this principle at work in the Prophets.

The key to interpreting the prophets' writings is understanding their ministries in the light of God's covenant with his people. Its provisions and prescriptions were enshrined in the canon of the law. The prophets were sent to warn the people that God would keep his written covenant word, even if that meant its judgments fell on them for their faithlessness and disobedience. The same God who spoke in the giving of the law now spoke again as he applied its covenant principles through the prophets.

The prophets' ministry, therefore, was to call God's people back to their covenant privileges and obligations, and thus to summon them back to live according to the divine canon written in the law. The same word of God could be heard in the sermons of the prophets as was heard in the writings of the law. 'Behold', said God to Jeremiah, 'I have put my words in your mouth.' [4] Thus through the prophets the divine canon was being applied. It was also being expanded.

[1] *Josh.* 1:7-9.
[2] *Exod.* 24:7. Bible comes from the Greek word for book: *biblos*.
[3] *Deut.* 31:26.
[4] *Jer.* 1:9.

The Hebrew canon also placed Joshua, Judges, Samuel, and Kings in the category of *prophecy*. These books interpreted history not from a 'neutral' point of view,[1] but from the perspective of the covenant canon of God's word. They read it through the lens of the covenant bond and law of God: faith and obedience leads to blessing; faithlessness and disobedience leads to the judgment curse.

In one sense then, the preaching of prophets like Elijah and Elisha was simply the tip of the iceberg. God was always assessing his people in the light of their response to the covenant canon—even when he sent no preachers to remind them that they were rebelling against him. God's canonical word was enough. Two ways were always set before the people: faith or unbelief, obedience or disobedience. Two consequences were always promised to follow: life or death, blessing or cursing.[2] It is in this sense that the prophets not only 'foretold' but 'forth-told' the word of God.

So two major sections were present in the enlarged 'canon' God was giving to his people. There was the Law contained in the first five books, and building on it, the Prophets.

As God's purposes unfolded and his Spirit continued to work, new material was added. For God's revelation was ongoing and progressive. Thus the canon included the books that came to be known collectively as 'The Writings': Psalms and Proverbs (both of which illustrate the covenant life style), Job, Daniel, Ezra and Nehemiah, Chronicles, as well as Ruth, Song of Solomon, Ecclesiastes, Lamentations, and Esther.

These last five books (known as The Five Scrolls) were for many centuries associated with the great Jewish Festivals. They were publicly read on such occasions, and used as illustrations of the ways of God with men. They were graphic illustrations of the covenant principles expounded in the Law and reinforced in the Prophets.

There is much that remains obscure about the way in which these particular books came to be regarded as part of the canon. What is clear is that by Jesus' time God's people recognised that in and through

---

[1] In fact there is no 'neutral' point of view, since interpretation always presupposes and involves a frame of reference in which it takes place.

[2] See *Deut.* 27-30 for a foundational exposition of this principle. Cf. also *Deut.* 30:19-20. *Psa.* 1 is an expression of this same covenant principle at work, and one reason it is placed first in the Book of Psalms.

these varied books the same voice of God was heard. Despite differences in authorship, style, type of literature, and time of composition, there was a unifying thread running through them all—the same covenant principles which God had given to the people at Sinai were demonstrated and illustrated in this diverse library of writings.

However, against the background of the complex issue of the development of the Old Testament canon there is an additional principle that simplifies matters. The Old Testament which we have is the Old Testament Jesus himself used, believed, and regarded as 'the mouth of God'.[1] He freely quoted various parts of the Old Testament as the word of God or Scripture. We may therefore safely receive its thirty-nine books as the word of God.

Jesus' view of the Old Testament

Our Lord clearly shared the view of his contemporaries that the Old Testament was divinely inspired and fully and finally authoritative. He was not at loggerheads with them over the contents (canon) of Scripture, but its interpretation.

Jesus spoke of the divine origin of the Pentateuch.[2] He constantly referred to the fulfilment of prophecy as a divine necessity;[3] he commented on the way in which David's writing was inspired by the Spirit.[4]

There was one specific time in our Lord's ministry when his deepest convictions about the Bible were most likely to come to the surface—when he was under the immense pressures of Gethsemane and Calvary. It is precisely then that he most clearly affirmed its authority in his own life:

• Why must he die? 'The Son of Man will go *just as it is written* about him' (*Matt.* 26:24).

• Why must he be betrayed? 'This is *to fulfil the Scripture:* "He who shares my bread has lifted up his heel against me"' (*John* 13:18).

---

[1] *Matt.* 4:4, citing *Deut.* 8:3.

[2] The Pentateuch refers to the first five books of the Bible. See *Matt.* 19:4-5. In *Matt.* 5:21-48 Jesus is contrasting traditions with Old Testament teaching, not denying the latter.

[3] For example, *Matt.* 26:54.

[4] *Mark* 12:36.

• Why must he be left alone? *'For it is written:* "I will strike the shepherd and the sheep will be scattered"' (*Mark* 14:27).

• Why must he be so hated? *'To fulfil what is written in their Law:* "They hated me without reason"' (*John* 15:25).

• Why does he not use his power to escape the cross? *'How then would the Scriptures be fulfilled* that say it must happen in this way?' (*Matt.* 26:54)

These words reflect the profoundest convictions of Jesus. We can be very confident that he held the Scriptures to be the inspired and inviolable word of God. For him what they said was what God said. Whatever his personal inclinations might be (and his cry in Gethsemane, 'Father, if it is possible, let this cup pass from me' indicates where his holy, human desires lay), he always bowed to Scripture as God's word and humbly submitted himself to it. He was the Man who lived not by bread alone but by every word that proceeds from the mouth of God.[1]

When the risen Christ met the two disciples on the Emmaus Road he reminded them of the words of 'Moses and all the Prophets' and explained how their words were fulfilled in his coming.[2] Later that evening, he made more explicit reference to the threefold division of the Old Testament:

> 'This is what I told you while I was still with you: Everything must be fulfilled that is written about me in the Law of Moses, the Prophets and the Psalms.' Then he opened their minds so that they could understand the Scriptures.[3]

It can hardly be accidental that Jesus' approach to the Scriptures in his state of exaltation, now raised from the dead, is identical to the view he consistently expressed in the period of his humiliation. Whatever Paul means by saying that in the incarnation our Lord 'made himself nothing',[4] he did not mean that he simply accepted his contemporaries' view of the Bible (even if false). If that had been the

[1] *Luke* 4:4, quoted from *Deut.* 8:3.
[2] *Luke* 24:27.
[3] *Luke* 24:44-45 NIV.
[4] *Phil.* 2:7.

case, his view of Scripture in his state of exaltation in the resurrection would surely not have been identical.

Jesus did not say: 'Forget about your Old Testament readings now that I am alive!' On the contrary, he continued to emphasise the absolute authority of God's word. He encouraged his disciples to understand it and to believe its testimony. In fact it was only *after* Jesus explained the message of the Bible to them that they began to understand who he was!

The Bible with which Jesus was familiar was not one book, but many scrolls.[1] The books were in a different order from ours; but the content was the same, and on that content he stamped his own imprimatur: 'This is the word of the Lord.' He viewed the books of the Old Testament as one unified Scripture that could not be broken.[2]

What the church's Lord thought of as God's word his church may confidently call 'the word of God' also. For at the end of the day Jesus himself is the canon of the Christian church.

The New Testament canon

It is often said that if the apostles knew how closely their writings are studied today, almost two thousand years after their deaths, they would be astonished. After all, were they not simply writing for their contemporaries?

The apostles were indeed writing *to* their first readers. But they were not writing only *for* them.

The apostles did not know how long it would be until Christ returned. But they were very conscious that God was speaking through them. They believed that what they were writing carried his authority. They knew that a major part of their commission was to give God's word to the world until the return of Christ.[3] The logic of the Great Commission virtually required them to write the New Testament. Without it the gospel might well have been totally corrupted within a couple of generations. How otherwise could the gospel have reached the ends of the earth and continue to do so to the end of the age?

[1] *Luke* 4:16-17.
[2] *John* 10:35. Notice the reference to a single entity which Jesus calls 'Scripture'.
[3] *Matt.* 28:18-20.

The mind of the apostles

The authors of the New Testament were also aware that what they wrote was not merely an expression of their personal witness to Christ. They believed that what they said and wrote was to be heard and read as God's word.

For example, Paul tells the young Christians at Thessalonica: 'I put you under oath before the Lord to have this letter read to all the brothers.'[1] He writes similarly to the Colossians: 'And when this letter has been read among you, have it also read in the church of the Laodiceans; and see that you also read the letter from Laodicea.'[2]

It would be marvellous to be able to identify 'the letter from Laodicea'.[3] Whatever it was, clearly Paul believed his writings should be read in the church in the same way the Old Testament was read in the synagogue—as the word of God on a par with the Old Testament Scriptures.

Imagine a church service where the Scripture reading is introduced with the words 'Let us hear the word of God.' The reader then says, 'The first reading from Scripture is taken from Isaiah 53.' And then he adds: 'The second reading is from a poem by T. S. Eliot.' Why would this jar on the emotions of a Christian? Because these two readings do not belong together as 'the word of God'. They do not have the same authority. By contrast Paul commanded the Thessalonians *under oath* to read his letters in the worship services alongside the word of God—because they were the word of God.[4]

At the end of the Letter to the Romans there is another statement which lends weight to this perspective. Speaking of the gospel of Christ, Paul says that it is an expression of

> the mystery that was kept secret for long ages but has now been disclosed and through the prophetic writings has been made known to all nations, according to the command of

---

[1] *1 Thess.* 5:27.

[2] *Col.* 4:16.

[3] It seems certain that this was a letter written by Paul. How would he know about it otherwise? Was this letter lost? Or was it perhaps a version of Ephesians sent to Laodicea which would have been taken along with Colossians on the journey through Ephesus, and Laodicea to Colossae?

[4] *2 Thess.* 2:15. For the public reading of Scripture see *1 Tim.* 4:13; *Rev.* 1:3.

the eternal God, to bring about the obedience of faith—to the only wise God be glory for evermore through Jesus Christ! Amen.[1]

These words are reminiscent of what he also wrote in Ephesians 3:3-6 about the revelation God had given to him. That revelation is now written down and is contained in 'prophetic writings'. The expression indicates that Paul realised the significance of what he himself was writing and believed it should he heard as the word of God coming through the mouth of a man.

The same sense of divine authority appears towards the close of Paul's lengthy discussion of the place and use of spiritual gifts:

> If anyone thinks that he is a prophet, or spiritual, he should acknowledge that the things I am writing to you are a command of the Lord. If anyone does not recognise this, he is not recognised.[2]

The test of true spirituality is not the exercise of spiritual gifts, but the recognition that the word of the apostolic letter is also the word of the Lord! It is difficult to imagine a stronger affirmation of the authority of the apostolic writings.

Similar claims appear in the correspondence to Thessalonica:

> And we also thank God constantly for this, that when you received the word of God, which you heard from us, you accepted it not as the word of men but as what it really is, the word of God, which is at work in you believers.[3]

> If anyone does not obey what we say in this letter, take note of that person, and have nothing to do with him, that he may be ashamed.[4]

Why should this not surprise us? Because when Jesus chose his apostles he had in view their specific role of adding to Scripture.

[1] *Rom.* 16:25-27.
[2] *1 Cor.* 14:37-38.
[3] *1 Thess.* 2:13.
[4] *2 Thess.* 3:14.

The role of the apostles

The word 'apostle' is derived from the Greek verb to send (*apostellō*). It carries the sense of being commissioned—an apostle is a person who has been given a commission by another.

In the Jewish tradition such a person was called a *shaliach*—a person who acted as an official representative or agent for someone else. He possessed what we would call a 'power of attorney'.[1] It was said that a person's *shaliach* (= *apostolos*) was as the person himself.[2]

The two (apparently contradictory) accounts of the healing of the centurion's servant in Matthew and Luke provide a perfect illustration of this concept. Matthew writes that a centurion came to Jesus, asked him to heal his servant, and engaged him in conversation.[3] In striking contrast, Luke says that the centurion sent some of the elders from the synagogue he had built to ask for Jesus' help.[4] Was Luke correcting Matthew on the basis of new evidence?

Why are these passages not blatantly contradicting each other? If we are familiar with the cultural role of the *shaliach* the answer is fairly straightforward. The elders came to Jesus *in the name of the centurion*. They were his *shaliachim*. They had authority to speak and act for him. 'A man's *shaliach* is as the man himself.' Their word was his word. They were his apostles. To listen to them was to listen to him. To deal with him was to deal with them.

The Apostle and his apostles

Jesus himself was the apostle[5] or *shaliach* of his Father.[6] In the same

---

[1] In the Septuagint (Greek) translation of the Old Testament, the Hebrew verb *shalach* is translated by *apostellō* about 700 times. Thus *apostolos* = *shaliach*.

[2] In *Gen.* 24:1-9 Abraham's trusted elderly servant clearly fulfils the role of a *shaliach* when he is sent to find a wife for Isaac.

[3] *Matt.* 8:5-13.

[4] *Luke* 7:1-10.

[5] *Heb.* 3:1.

[6] In order to feel the weight of significance the apostle John placed on Jesus authoritatively sending the apostles *as the one who was himself sent by the Father,* note: *John* 3:17, 34; 4:34; 5:23, 24, 20, 36, 37, 38; 6:29, 38, 39, 40, 44, 57; 7:16, 18, 28, 29, 33; 8:16, 18, 26, 29, 42; 9:7; 10:36; 11:42; 12:44, 45, 49; 13:20; 14:24; 15:21; 16:5; 17:3, 18, 21, 23, 25. This series of statements climaxes in 20:21: '"As the Father has sent me, even so I am sending you." And when he had said this he breathed on them and said to them, "Receive the Holy Spirit. If you forgive the sins of anyone, they are forgiven;

way, Jesus invested his apostles with his own authority. Jesus chose them with this in view:

> And he appointed twelve (whom he also named apostles) so that they might be with him and he might send them out to preach and have authority to cast out demons.[1]

He then explicitly prepared them to serve in this capacity.[2] 'Truly, truly, I say to you, whoever receives the one I send receives me, and whoever receives me receives the one who sent me'.[3]

This is part of the reason Paul defended his apostolic office so strongly.[4] He was not fixated on his personal reputation,[5] but deeply concerned that the Lord's word through him should be received and obeyed. He was just as clearly an apostle as others. The risen Christ had personally called and commissioned him as his *shaliach*.[6] His task was to convey the authoritative word of the Master, just as other apostles did.[7]

The author of Hebrews compares the apostles with the angels who were the go-betweens in the giving of the law at Sinai.[8] This eloquently expresses their role in bringing the new word of God to the new people of God. So, when John wrote his Gospel he used the same expression to describe his own writing as he had done for the books of the Old Testament—'it is written'[9]

Against this background, and building on this foundation, it is possible for the apostle Peter to say:

> And count the patience of our Lord as salvation, just as our beloved brother Paul also wrote to you according to the wisdom given him, as he does in all his letters when he speaks in them of these matters. There are some things in them that

---

if you withhold forgiveness from anyone, it is withheld.'" The extent to which the apostles are granted 'power of attorney' could hardly be more powerfully stated.

[1] *Mark* 3:14.

[2] *Matt.* 10:1, 5; *Luke* 9:1-10.

[3] *John* 13:20.

[4] See *1 Cor.* 9:1 ff; *Gal.* 1:1; 11-24.

[5] For example, *2 Cor.* 11 and 12.

[6] *Gal.* 1:11-12. He was 'apostled' to preach the gospel, *1 Cor.* 1:17.

[7] See. *Matt.* 10:40; *John* 13:20; 14:26; 15:26; 16:13-15; *Acts* 1:2.

[8] *Heb.* 2:2.

[9] *John* 20:31; cf. *John* 2:17; 6:31, 45; 10:34; 12:14; 15:25.

are hard to understand, which the ignorant and unstable twist to their own destruction, as they do *the other Scriptures*.[1]

Here Peter places Paul's letters on the same level as 'the other Scriptures'. The implication is that the writings which God had given to the church through him—and by parity of reasoning, the other apostles too—were already being regarded as part of Scripture. Similarly Paul cites both Deuteronomy 25:4 and Luke 10:7 under the rubric 'for the Scripture says …'.[2]

As we have seen already, Jesus prepared the apostles for this ministry.[3] This made them unique witnesses to him. Others could speak of his saving power; others could be evangelists, pastors and teachers. But they had received the special promise that he would send his Spirit to them to equip them to serve as his *shaliachim*.[4] He gave them his authority to give the church its rule of faith and life. He had all authority in heaven and earth; they were therefore to go, in his authority, to teach the nations everything he had taught them.

Ultimately, therefore, the authority of the New Testament rests on the authority of Jesus himself.

Jesus promised that the Spirit would bear witness to him through the witness of the apostles. The Spirit is also seen as Jesus' divine *shaliach*, sent by the Father in his name.[5] Since both the Spirit and the apostles were with Jesus 'from the beginning' (the Spirit from the beginning of his whole life; the apostles from the beginning of his ministry) their joint witness possesses both authenticity and divine authority.[6] The Spirit would lead the apostles into all truth. He would

---

[1] *2 Pet.* 3:15-16.

[2] *1 Tim.* 5:18.

[3] See above, pp. 14-17.

[4] Clearly this did not imply that all the apostles would be 'writing apostles' any more than all of the prophets were necessarily 'writing prophets'. Rather, Jesus was commissioning the apostles as the 'new scripture-giving community'. For this reason in the early church the recognition of a book's canonicity seems to have been intimately related to it emerging from the apostolic community (as in the case of Luke's Gospel because of the author's relationship to Paul, and Mark's Gospel because of his relationship to Peter). Interestingly the words in *Heb.* 2:2 which are usually understood to exclude apostolic authorship, at the same time underline the author's intimacy with the apostolic community.

[5] *John* 14:16, 26.

[6] *John* 15:26-27.

'not speak on his own authority, but whatever he hears he will speak, and he will declare to you the things that are to come'.[1]

These are truly remarkable words. They reveal a 'chain of authority' in God's revelation in his word. The Father sends the Son, the Son sends the Spirit, the Spirit empowers the apostles and through them the word of God comes to us. But *how* did this word come to us?

People become Christians in different ways—some in the context of a Christian home, others through a friend, others at meetings where the gospel was explained, yet others by reading a Christian book privately. Ultimately all these sources have one origin: the New Testament. As we have seen its contents are perfectly summarised by the three categories Jesus mentioned to the apostles. He will give them the Holy Spirit so that they will be able to:

(1) Remember and communicate what he had taught them (Gospels and to some extent Acts);

(2) Lead them into all the truth about him (Letters); and

(3) Show them the things that were still to come (prophecies and the book of Revelation).

In essence, without actually saying it in so many words, Jesus is explaining: 'My apostles will write the New Testament.'

In writing the New Testament, then, the apostles were simply fulfilling an essential aspect to the Great Commission to go into all the world and bring the gospel to every creature, making disciples and baptizing them, and then teaching them everything the Lord Jesus taught them until the end of the age (*Matt.* 28:18-20).

These words were spoken exclusively to the apostles (neither you nor I were there!). How could the twelve go to the end of the earth and the end of the age? Only if their witness became a permanent record. Thus it is through their writing of the New Testament that we today, and millions of believers since the days of the apostles, have 'believed' through the apostles' word.[2]

---

[1] *John* 16:12-15.
[2] *John* 17:20.

It takes time

God committed his word to writing through different individuals, at different times, and in different places. Inevitably it took some time before all the churches in every part of the evangelised world recognised the twenty-seven books of the New Testament as God's word. It could not have been any other way, since it took time for each church to come into possession of all of the books of the New Testament.[1]

At first churches possessed only one book of the New Testament. Gradually these books were shared and collected. The Colossian church had two of Paul's letters.[2] What we might call 'mini-versions' of the New Testament must have been formed. Peter's comment on Paul's letters in 2 Peter 3:15-16 suggests that numbers of churches already possessed collections of them. In this sense, for a temporary period, different parts of the whole 'canon' of the New Testament must have been present in various parts of the world.

It is not surprising then that it was some time before all the churches had equal access to all of the apostolic writings. Inevitably the recognition of the whole canon by the entire church took place slowly. Apart from anything else, simply imagine the logistical complexities of all the churches communicating with each other to ask: 'What's in your congregation's New Testament?' What is, however, impressively true is that from the earliest period the entire Christian church recognised that God had been adding to his word through the apostles.

We know from the citations in the work of Irenaeus of Lyons[3] that by the late second century almost all of the New Testament books must have been widely received as Scripture. By the end of the fourth century it was universally acknowledged that the books we now call the New Testament were the word of God for the new age of the gospel.[4]

[1] Interestingly while this happened in a world in which scrolls were typically used, Christians appear to have used the codex (book) format to a much greater extent, suggestive of their sense that these writings belonged together as a single canon.

[2] *Col.* 4:16.

[3] Irenaeus (c. A.D. 130–200) was bishop of the church at Lyons. His writings include references to all of the New Testament books with the exceptions of *2 Pet.*, *3 John*, and *Heb.*

[4] In the East the recognition of the canon as we know it is associated with The

It may help clarify this issue if we distinguish four 'moments' in the story of the church's recognition of the canon of the New Testament:

(1) The 'moment' at which a book of the New Testament was written and became immediately canonical (*i.e.* 'became' Scripture);

(2) The 'moment' at which this book was read by the church for whom it was written and was received as the canonical word of God;

(3) The 'moment' at which a book written for one group of Christians was shared and used by other churches as canonical Scripture;

(4) The 'moment' at which it was possible for all the churches to possess all of the apostolic writings and as a community give public recognition to the New Testament canon as a whole.

Strictly speaking the books became part of the canon the moment the ink dried on the page. They were breathed out by God. They were God's word. But only when gathered together over an extended period was it possible for any church, and then for the entire church, to recognise them as a whole as the canon.

It should not disturb us that the recognition of the New Testament canon took time. The only alternative to such a process would have been for it to have been written by one man, or by several men writing in the same place simultaneously. But such a book, or compilation of simultaneously written books, would have had a very different content from the new Scriptures God actually gave to the church.

It should be clear, therefore, that the church did not *create* the canon. Yes, it reached agreement on what books formed the canon of the New Testament. But in doing so it was *recognising* that these books were canonical, not *making* them so.

In summary, then, God breathed out, through human authors, twenty-seven new books which he intended should complete the canon of Scripture. He did this through different authors, at different times, and in different places. Because of that—as is true of the Old Testament Scriptures—there are questions about the process we are simply not able to answer. Did Paul write other letters that are *not* in the New Testament? 1 Corinthians 5:9 suggests that he did.

Thirty-ninth Paschal Letter of Athanasius written in A.D. 367 and in the West with the Council of Carthage in A.D. 397.

Did other apostles write letters that were not circulated or preserved? Was John familiar with all of the other twenty-six books in our New Testament and realise, when he was writing Revelation, that this was the last book?

We cannot answer all of these questions with certainty. What is clear, however, is that God superintended not only the writing but the preservation of the canonical books 'by His singular care and providence'.[1] Having given his word to the church, and preserved his word for the church, he has guided the church to recognise and receive it 'as what it really is, the word of God'.[2]

What relevance does this have for us today, if any?

Authority, sufficiency, finality

If God has given us the Scriptures to be the canon or rule for our lives, it follows that we must regard them as the *supreme authority* for our lives. Paul tells us that they are 'breathed out' by God. There can be no more authoritative word than one that comes to us on divine breath.

The Scriptures are also a *sufficient authority* for the whole of the Christian life. They are 'profitable for teaching, for reproof, for correction, and for training in righteousness, that the man of God may be competent, *equipped for every good work*'.[3]

The Scriptures do not tell us everything about everything. They provide no instruction about computer programming, or how best to organise a library, the correct way to swing a golf club, or how to play chess. They do not tell us how far away the sun is from the earth, what DNA is, how best to remove an appendix surgically, the best coffee to drink, or the name of the person we should marry.

That is not an expression of any deficiency on their part. For there is a focus and a goal to the sufficiency of the Scriptures. Everything I need to learn in order to live to the glory of God and enjoy him for ever I will find in the application of Scripture.

Yet this narrow focus broadens out into everything. For one thing, Scripture teaches us something about everything. Since the Bible gives us grounds for believing we live in a *uni*verse, Christians understand

[1] *The Confession of Faith*, I.8.
[2] *1 Thess.* 2:13.
[3] *2 Tim.* 3:16.

that everything has the characteristic of createdness, of derivativeness, and also that everything fits into the grand design of God.

So Scripture is sufficient to give me a rational ground for thinking about anything and everything on the assumption that this world and everything in it make sense. Further, no matter what my calling or abilities, the Scriptures are sufficient to teach me principles that will enable me to think and act in a God-honouring way when I am engaged in any activity or vocation.

Inerrancy

In this context it is appropriate for us to ask an important and much-debated question: If Scripture is our final authority, exactly how reliable is it as the authority on which we should base the whole of our lives?

If, convinced that the Bible is the word of God, we ask that question from a *theological* point of view there seems to be only one reasonable answer: Scripture is completely reliable. For the God who has 'breathed out' Scripture is trustworthy in everything he does and says. He is the God who cannot lie;[1] he speaks the truth in everything he says.[2] The notion that he would be untruthful and err is contradictory to everything Scripture tells us about him.

However, Scripture also tells us that the word of God comes through the minds and mouths of men. Does this not mean that it will inevitably contain some mistakes? After all, 'To err is human.' If so, to use an old illustration, is it not more appropriate to think of the Bible as though it were a slightly scratched gramophone record? Or, in more contemporary terms, is the Bible not like a digitized version of an old recording—despite deficiencies, the music can still be heard, and if we listen with care we can make out the words quite well.

But two obvious considerations need to be remembered.

First, strictly speaking, 'to err' is not so much *human* as it is *fallen.*

Second, not everything said by humans involves error. Life revolves round the fact that people speak the truth, that what they say is not riddled with mistakes. A person can go through the whole day without making a single erroneous statement. And societies function well only where a premium is placed on truth telling. Much of what we say and write is, in a fairly obvious sense, error free.

[1] *Titus* 1:2; *Heb.* 6:18, cf. *Num.* 23:19.
[2] *Prov.* 30:5.

It is surely then within the power of God to preserve the authors of Scripture from error.

So *the assumption that the Scriptures inevitably contain errors because written by men is false.*

But there is a further consideration, in addition to that of the logic of our theology. The books of Scripture specifically affirm the truthfulness of what is written; those who appear in their narratives share that perspective. Jesus himself spoke of God's word as 'truth'. Almost in passing he stated that 'Scripture cannot be broken'[1]—and it is often in such passing comments that our real convictions come to the surface.

Other passages in Scripture point us in the same direction. The New Testament authors refer to passages and authors in the Old Testament in a way that assumes their trustworthiness and absolute reliability. There is no New Testament example of an author taking the view that there were probably, or even possibly, errors of any kind in Scripture. For them if Scripture said it, then God said it; when he put his words into men's mouths those words could be trusted fully and regarded as accurate. This applies both to statements of facts and to interpretations of events. The Scriptures are inerrant.

But when we speak about the 'inerrancy' of the Bible, what do we mean? 'Inerrancy' is, after all, a privative term. It tells us what Scripture is not—it is in-, or non-, errant, that is, 'error free'. What kind of 'inerrancy' do we mean?

A false alternative?

Before we think further about this, however, there is a much discussed issue we ought to address. By no means all Christians (indeed by no means all Christians who describe the Bible as the word of God) share the view that it is 'inerrant'. Many prefer the term 'infallible' believing that although Scripture may contain errors of fact, its message of salvation will not fail us. But this is a sleight of hand so long as our dictionaries explain 'infallible' and 'inerrant' in mutual terms.

Frequently, however, we are told that the term 'inerrant' has an Achilles' heel, since it needs to be *qualified* in order to explain exactly what it means. If so, then the term itself, it is argued, is surely an unhelpful one. From this point of view the term 'infallible' is both better, and, it is claimed, uses the historic term to present the historic

[1] *John* 10:35.

view of the church. 'Inerrant', the argument often continues, is (i) a relatively recent concept and (ii) has come into popular use largely because of the influence of the influential American theologians Charles Hodge and Benjamin B. Warfield, both of whom taught at Princeton Theological Seminary.

Granted that, for example, the *Westminster Confession of Faith* uses the term 'infallible' to describe the Bible,[1] the power of this argument lies more in its rhetoric than in its substance.

1. For one thing, to argue that the term 'inerrant' is unhelpful because it needs to be qualified is naive.

'Qualify' is a grammatical term. Every schoolboy of my generation learned from *The Approach to Standard English* that 'an adjective qualifies a noun'—it tells us something about its quality.

Say, for example, I play golf and want to purchase a new set of golf clubs. All golf clubs have shafts. The manufacturer asks me: 'What shafts do you need in your clubs—"senior" or "regular" or "stiff" or perhaps "extra stiff"?' If I say, 'Look, these qualifying terms are unhelpful. If you have to qualify "shaft" in these different ways, you shouldn't use it!' But the club-maker will reply: 'Sir, you don't understand. These qualifications clarify. If you are going to hit a golf ball with a club you will soon see the importance of these qualifications!'

The same is true when we describe the inerrancy of Scripture.

2. To say that, because the term 'inerrant' needs to be qualified, the term 'infallible' is preferable, is also naive thinking. For the term 'infallibility' equally needs to be qualified, and often for exactly the same reasons and in exactly the same way as 'inerrancy'. This criticism involves a self-defeating principle. For we are bound to ask: 'What do you mean by "infallibility"? When you say "Scripture is infallible" do you mean "error-free" (with the *Oxford English Dictionary*), or what? Is Scripture "infallible" on all matters, or only some? Is it "infallible" in historical detail, and in scientific issues, or is the infallibility linked only to what it says about God?' Some authors who reject inerrancy in favour of infallibility believe there are errors of fact and obvious inconsistencies in Scripture. For that very reason, when someone says Scripture is 'infallible', there is all the more reason to ask for clarification, *i.e.* qualification.

[1] The *Confession* speaks of 'the infallible truth and divine authority' of Scripture, I.v.

The point being established here is a simple, but important one: the criticism that the term 'inerrant' needs to be qualified and *therefore* is inadequate has no real substance. Qualifying a term clarifies it. Indeed rather than weaken, qualifying it may actually strengthen a term.

3. It is true that the term 'inerrancy' has been much more prominent in North America than, say, in the United Kingdom. But given the massive number of Christians, the much greater number and faculty size of major evangelical seminaries in the United States and the number of publications that flow from them, this is hardly surprising. What is surprising is the implication that inerrancy is (i) essentially an *American* peculiarity and (ii) one of relatively recent vintage and (iii) largely thrust into the atmosphere by two, albeit hugely influential, American theologians and their colleagues.

Even if this were true, it could hardly be grounds for rejecting the term. Christians in the fourth century did not reject the term *homoousios*[1] simply because it was not traditional terminology.

But in fact these claims can be dismissed. Perhaps the most interesting way of doing so is found in the following quotation which affirms the inerrancy of Scripture:

> It is absolutely wrong ... either to narrow inspiration to certain parts of Scripture or to admit that the sacred writer has erred ... So far is it from being possible that any error can co-exist with inspiration, that inspiration not only is essentially incompatible with error, but excludes and rejects it as absolutely and necessarily as it is impossible that God himself, the Supreme Truth, can utter that which is not true.

The author? It certainly sounds like an early twentieth-century statement that might be found in one or other of the essays on Scripture written by the American theologian, B. B. Warfield. But its source is a diameter removed. For

(i) the statement comes from the work of a European theologian, not an American one.

(ii) the statement was not made by an evangelical theologian.

(iii) the statement was originally written in Latin, not in English.

---

[1] 'Of the same substance' (*i.e.* with the Father)—the term employed by the Council of Nicaea (A.D. 325) to indicate the full and true deity of the Lord Jesus.

(iv) the statement was published in 1893.

(v) the statement appears in *Providentissimus Deus,* the Papal Encyclical of Leo XIII issued in that year.

This is simply one example from the history of theology giving the lie to the notion that inerrancy is a recent evangelical invention. Rather inerrancy is the classical doctrine of the church, and not the idiosyncratic view of a narrow band of modern theologians. While the interpretation of Scripture may have been debated in the historic controversies of the church, and the sufficiency of Scripture may have been an issue at the time of the Reformation, the historic view of the Christian church is that the Scriptures themselves are without error. Indeed this is actually what the term 'infallibility' denoted through the history of the church.

In fact while the words have different nuances they function as synonyms for each other. At the very least the two terms are interchangeable. Thus, for example, the *Oxford English Dictionary* defines 'infallible' as 'incapable of erring'. Indeed, it could be argued that, if anything, the term 'infallible' is the stronger, not the weaker of the two.

Qualifying descriptions

It is important to 'qualify' terms. What do we mean—and not mean—by 'inerrant'? In what sense is Scripture without error in what it affirms?

(1) When we refer to the Bible as 'inerrant' we are, of course, ultimately referring to the text of the Old Testament as it was received by Jesus, and the text of the New Testament as it was written by the apostles. Why is this important since we do not possess what are often referred to as 'the original autographs'?

We know that during the process of copying, whether from one manuscript to another by an individual, or many manuscripts dictated to scribes writing simultaneously, errors can creep in to the copies. If you think about it, very few readers of a book have seen its 'original autograph'. As far as I am aware, the 'original autograph' of the first edition of this book is no longer in existence. That notwithstanding, it remains the text I originally wrote. The fact that I no longer have it does not make it irrelevant. It is what I wrote.

Even with modern technology we find errors in the published versions of books which were absent from the original autograph. Until the fourteenth century, book production was much more error prone. They were copied by hand. Sometimes they were dictated to a group of scribes. Errors caused by mis-hearing easily crept in. Nor is it surprising if a copyist wrote down a wrong word from a manuscript as his eyes moved from the original to the copy he was writing.

Similar slips take place today. I recall writing the words: 'Rend your heart and not your garments' (*Joel* 2:13) in a manuscript. When the manuscript came back to me for review the wrong substitution of one letter (a 't' instead of a 'd'), changed my meaning dramatically, and humorously: '*Rent* your heart, and not your garments.' That may be good advice; but it was not what my 'autographic text' said! I didn't say: 'I no longer have the "autographic text"—it doesn't matter.'

The reason for speaking of the inerrancy of the text of the Old Testament Jesus used and the autographic texts of the apostles should be well understood by every author.

(2) When we speak of the 'inerrancy' of the Bible we realize that Scripture needs to be interpreted properly, in a manner that is sensitive to its various genres and styles. It should be read in its own terms and not according to inappropriate standards. A young male student of astronomy is not likely to criticize an attractive young female doctoral student in English poetry who asks: 'Would you like to go for a walk round campus *before sunset?*' Even astronomers speak in those terms.

It should be obvious that the Bible was not written to be a twenty-first century scientific textbook. A moment's reflection indicates that, if it were, its precision and detail would (a) be incomprehensible to the vast majority of readers, and (b) very soon be out of date! So we ought to assess the Bible by appropriate standards, not inappropriate ones.

(3) The history recorded in Scripture is written from a different perspective from that of technical historians today.

Biblical authors believed that history is the unfolding of God's purposes and reveals the outworking of his promises. It has a meaning written into it, and a goal to which it is moving. By contrast, contemporary historians tend to completely exclude God from history. For all practical purposes they adopt the view that while they may be able to trace causes and effects in the events that transpire it is no part of their discipline to discern an underlying plot line, or a divine plan and purpose, or for that matter an ultimate goal in history. It should not therefore surprise us that the authors of Scripture both describe and assess historical events very differently.

(4) We recognize that the inerrancy of Scripture is, in the nature of the case, not something we can 'prove'. We do not know enough about the past to enable us to prove that all the Bible's statements are true; we do not know what will happen in the future to be able to verify any of its prophecies in advance. Our conviction is rooted in the more basic belief that the Bible is the word of God and that every indication we have confirms its reliability as such. There may remain elements in Scripture that we are not able to 'piece together'; but in the light of all we know about the Bible and its authors we see no reason to doubt its reliability.

Critics of inerrancy point to what they regard as inconsistencies or contradictions in the text to demonstrate their perspective. For example, as we have already seen, in one Gospel a Roman centurion asks Jesus to heal his servant while in another it is the elders of the local synagogue who come to speak to him. But far from being a contradiction, in this instance some knowledge of the cultural context enables us to see that these accounts are in fact completely harmonious.[1]

Again, Jesus healed the blind as he made his way through Jericho to Jerusalem. But there are differences in the Gospel accounts. Did Jesus heal *two blind men* as he *left* Jericho (*Matt.* 20:29-30)? Or only *one blind man* as he *left* Jericho (*Mark* 10:46)? Or *one blind man* as he *entered* Jericho (*Luke* 18:35)? It may be easy enough to say: 'If he healed two, then he healed one. Surely all we have here is the different focus of the Gospel writers?' But aren't entering and leaving antithetical ideas? One cannot both enter and leave at the same time! Unless of course there was a larger area called 'Jericho' that one entered as one left the city called 'Jericho'. Or perhaps there were two healings? If so the similarity between them, even in the words spoken, is hardly surprising. Either explanation is surely more likely than that one Gospel writer consciously contradicted the other.

Entire volumes have been written on these and similar passages suggesting resolutions to the difficulties some feel with them.[2] But as

---

[1] See above, p. 31.

[2] Including Gleason Archer, *Encyclopaedia of Bible Difficulties*, (Grand Rapids, Zondervan, 1982).

we have seen, our conviction of the inspiration and reliability of the Bible is not based on our ability to prove the doctrine of inerrancy by showing that every statement in Scripture is error-free, but by a Spirit-born recognition of the divine character of Scripture. Like the biblical teaching on the virgin conception, the resurrection, and the return of Christ, inerrancy is an article of faith.

Finality

There is also a *finality* about the New Testament Scriptures. Since they record God's last word for the last days, we should not now expect that God will 'speak' to us directly. Now that he has spoken in Christ and through the apostles we discover his will by applying Scripture to all the varied circumstances in which we live. We do not expect, for example, that God will whisper to us the name of the person we are to marry, the calling we are to pursue, the church to which we are to belong, or the place we should live. We discover God's will in these areas by the careful and ongoing application of the principles, commands, and illustrations we find in Scripture to the life-situations in which we find ourselves.[1]

This is an obvious implication of having the completed canon of Scripture. It might seem hardly worth mentioning were it not for the fact that it has become commonplace among contemporary Christians to believe God speaks to us *apart from and in addition to* his word.

The more balanced representatives of this view emphasise that this does not mean *in contradiction of* God's word. But nevertheless, *in effect* this establishes the possibility in practice of a second 'canon', separate from, and additional to, Scripture. And frequently—indeed almost inevitably—this second stream of revelation becomes the practical rule that directs the Christian life.[2] It is seen as a more immediate and individualised revelation. These characteristics mean it is liable to be given precedence over the reading of, meditation on, reflection about, and application of the written Scriptures.

---

[1] I have expounded this in some detail in *Discovering God's Will* (Edinburgh: The Banner of Truth Trust, 1982, repr. 2013).

[2] By a strange twist the dynamics of this way of thinking are analogous to Roman Catholic teaching. The Roman Catholic Church teaches that while there is a single source for revelation (God), there are two streams by which it comes to us (Sacred Scripture and Sacred Tradition). Historically the latter, which on occasion adds to Scripture, has tended to become the practical canon for the life of the church.

Whenever someone prefaces a statement by 'the Lord told me' or 'the Spirit revealed to me' and is referring to anything other than Scripture they have in effect established a second canon for themselves, an *additional* stream of revelation. But, as William Bridge wisely noted, 'who doth not know that the Devil will speak an hundred Truths, that he may crowd in one lye amongst them'.[1]

At one time I was a regular customer of a very talkative hairdresser. She became a Christian—but remained very talkative! Customers now began to prefer a different hairdresser to avoid being confronted by the gospel!

After some time she told me how excited she was because her pastor was teaching her how to live so that every detail of her life could be directed by the Holy Spirit. This sounded wonderfully encouraging. But in fact her pastor had been teaching 'How to listen to what the Spirit is saying to you immediately, personally, and individually each day'. I recall her telling me with enthusiasm how she had learned to listen to the Spirit so that she would know whether he wanted her to put on the right foot sock or the left foot sock first in the morning.

But this pathway of pursuing detailed obedience to extra-biblical revelation always has the same tendency. One day it will lead to complete paralysis—not putting on either sock because the Spirit has not 'spoken'. Or it will lead to guilt when things go awry and then the individual fears that she may have disobeyed the Lord by putting on the wrong sock at the beginning of the day.

This is not to say that our inner promptings and 'feelings' are unimportant. They are, after all, superintended by the providential rule of God. But unlike Scripture, providential experiences do not come with their own built-in interpretation and we cannot claim for them 'thus says the Lord'. They are the result of processes within our own minds—even if they seem to come to us without prior conscious reflection.

The more our minds are saturated in Scripture the greater will be its impact on our mental processes at every level. Thus subjective feelings and judgments can be healthy expressions of the impact of biblical teaching on our responses to life situations. But our approach with

---

[1] William Bridge, *Scripture Light the Most Sure Light*, in *Twenty One Several Books of Mr William Bridge collected into two volumes* (London, 1656), vol. 2, p. 15.

everything that comes into our minds is to submit it to God's word in Scripture. It is our only safe guide.[1]

Understanding the authority and function of canonical Scripture—that God has adequately revealed his will for the church *in the Bible*—saves us from the instability of such 'bolt-from-the-blue' approaches to guidance. For all its apparent spirituality, immediacy is no guarantee of validity. And not every Christian is sufficiently mature enough to know how to distinguish the work of the Spirit from the influence of an enemy who appears as an angel of light.[2]

God has provided a safe and secure pathway for us in the directives, promises, examples, and commands of his written word. In their light we seek to interpret the significance of all his providences—including our mental processes and perceptions. Every thought we have about what *may be* the will of God we will want to bring to the touchstone of the teaching of the Bible.

This is the classical reformed view of the Bible, sometimes described as *Sola Scriptura* (Scripture alone). But it does not mean that God leaves us on our own. We discover the wonder of its truth not as isolated hermits but 'together with all the saints'![3]

We live in an age characterised by a reaction to sterile rationalism. We have a preference for, and have become used to, the immediate. There is therefore a subtle attraction about the subjective authority of personal experience in distinction from the objective authority of a book that needs to be studied and applied. All the more reason for us to be people of the Book who are growing in ability to apply its teaching to every life situation.

Instead of narrowing and confining life, biblical wisdom makes us strong and stable. Plus, unlike immediate guidance that bypasses Scripture completely, the patient study of God's written revelation gradually transforms our patterns of thinking and moulds our character. As we will see, it is in order to transform us by the renewing of our minds[4] that God has given us the Bible in the first place.

---

[1] I am grateful to the publishers for permission to include Professor John Murray's valuable discussion, 'The Guidance of the Holy Spirit', as Appendix A, pp. 183-187.

[2] *2 Cor.* 11:14.

[3] See Paul's prayer in *Eph.* 3:17-19.

[4] *Rom.* 12:1-2.

Thus, at the end of the day how we understand Scripture as our canon—our rule of faith and life—has very practical repercussions.

3. Is This God's Word?

W E have been discussing how the Bible came to be written. But if someone were to ask: 'How do you *know* that the Bible really is God's word?' how would you answer?

The message Paul brought to the Thessalonians was received 'not as the word of men, but as it actually is, the word of God, which is at work in you who believe'.[1] But how did *he* know that this was true, and what convinced the Thessalonians? And how can we find this kind of certainty about the written word, the Bible?

We come to believe that the books of the New Testament are God's word:

> • Because they express a self conscious awareness that they are God's word. In this sense they make a claim on us to believe that they are the word of God.

> • Because as we read them the conviction is born in us that this is indeed what they are.

Our conviction therefore arises from the objective witness of the Scriptures themselves and comes to expression in a subjective persuasion, produced in us by the Spirit as we read them, that they are the word of God.

Claims made by the Bible?

The Bible is a collection of volumes written at different times and gathered together over many centuries. But in another sense it is also a single book with a great central theme running through it. This dual

---

[1] *1 Thess.* 2:13.

dimension is explained by the fact that while it was written by many men at different times it has one ultimate source, God himself, who speaks through its many authors.

This is not merely an interpretation which the church has placed on the Bible, as though the church 'compiled' Scripture.[1] It comes to expression within the pages of the books of the Bible themselves.

When we expound Christian doctrines we develop them on the basis of what the Bible as a whole says about them. But is it really possible for us to do this with the Bible itself? Can we meaningfully speak of 'the Bible's view of itself'? After all, until the last sentence of the book of Revelation was written the Bible was incomplete. Nor does that last sentence tell us (1) the books that constitute the Bible, (2) that it is the last sentence in the Bible, and (3) that it, and all preceding sentences in the Bible, are God's word.

How then can the Bible speak about the nature of the Bible as a whole? The answer is that the books of the Bible (and therefore the Bible as a whole) display a consciousness of their own nature. As we have seen, the apostles were aware that God was adding to the canon of the Old Testament through them.

When Paul wrote that 'All Scripture is God-breathed'[2] he had the Old Testament primarily in mind. But his statement implies that every piece of writing that belongs to the category of 'Scripture' shares this characteristic. The 'sacred writings' which Timothy had known since infancy[3] were breathed out by God himself. But the apostles believed that what they wrote belonged to the same category, and actually contained superior revelation. The former revelation had been preliminary; the 'new' revelation in Christ was consummatory.

The apostles thus saw themselves as adding to 'what is written'. They were fully aware that they were passing on an authoritative message to the church. They understood that Jesus had placed his imprimatur upon the Old Testament as God's word. But in addition they knew that he had given them his imprimatur to add to and

---

[1] As we have already noted, the canon of the Bible was not created by the church. Rather its contents were the word of God at the point of writing. The process of 'canonization' of the books of the Bible is therefore one of recognising it, not creating it. God provided the canon, the church merely received it.

[2] *2 Tim.* 3:16.

[3] *2 Tim.* 3:14-15.

complete the already existing Scriptures. The Holy Spirit was given to them to enable them to accomplish this.[1] They were to take this new word of God into the world until the end of the age.[2] All this we have already noticed.

We must now go a step further and ask: How is it that the Bible produces its effect on us so that we believe its testimony to its God-given nature?

The effects of the Bible

The Bible is a wonderful book. There may have been a time when *The Thoughts of Chairman Mao* or even *Harry Potter* outsold copies of the *Authorised* (King James) *Version* of the Bible. But how short-lived are other best-sellers! The Bible has lasted, and stood the test of time. One reason is that it is great literature, widely acknowledged as the ultimate masterpiece. Its qualities make a unique impact on its readers.

Christians used to place considerable weight on this:

> Read Demosthenes or Cicero; read Plato, Aristotle, and others of that tribe. They will, I admit, allure you, delight you, move you, enrapture you in wonderful measure. But betake yourself from them to this sacred reading. Then, in spite of yourself, so deeply will it affect you, so penetrate your heart, so fix itself in your very marrow, that compared with its deep impression, such vigor as the orators and philosophers have will nearly vanish. Consequently it is easy to see that the Sacred Scriptures, which so far surpass all gifts and graces of human endeavour, breathe something divine.[3]

Today most of us do not find that the philosophers and orators of antiquity delight or enrapture us, and therefore this may seem a little exaggerated! But Calvin's point is valid nonetheless. There is something uniquely impressive about the Bible. To read it with an open mind is to be touched by its grandeur and power. Indeed a comparison of the books of the New Testament with even the literature produced shortly afterwards by Christians in the post-apostolic church underlines the vast difference between them.

[1] Cf. *John* 14:25, 26; 16:12-15.
[2] *Matt.* 28:18-20.
[3] John Calvin, *Institutes* I.viii.1.

The Westminster Confession expresses this well:

> And the heavenliness of the matter, the efficacy of the doctrine, the majesty of the style, the consent of all the parts, the scope of the whole (which is, to give all glory to God), the full discovery it makes of the only way of man's salvation, the many other incomparable excellencies, and the entire perfection thereof, are arguments whereby it doth abundantly evidence itself to be the Word of God.[1]

But there is more to the Bible's effect on us than this.

When the two disciples who met Jesus on the road to Emmaus later re-lived their experience, they discovered they had had identical reactions: when Jesus explained the message of the Old Testament their hearts had 'burned within' them.

This subjective impact has been repeated throughout the ages as God's word has been read and preached. John Wesley described it in almost identical terms.[2] He was present at a meeting in Aldersgate Street, London. Someone was reading Luther's introduction to Paul's Letter to the Romans. Wesley's heart was 'strangely warmed'.

This conviction that the Bible is the word of God arises from its nature as the word of God and the Spirit's persuading us that this is indeed what it is. Inner persuasion is the result. *The Westminster Confession* again well expresses this when it notes that the remarkable qualities of Scripture notwithstanding,

> our full persuasion and assurance of the infallible truth and divine authority thereof, is from the inward work of the Holy Spirit, bearing witness by and with the Word in our hearts.[3]

Theologians call this 'the testimony of the Holy Spirit'.

Abraham Kuyper, the multi-talented theologian who became Prime Minister of the Netherlands, was already a young minister before he experienced this himself. Here is his description of what happens:

> The veil is gradually pushed aside. The eye turns toward the Divine light that radiates from the Scripture, and now our

---

[1] *The Confession of Faith,* I:5.
[2] In his *Diary* for May 24, 1738.
[3] *loc. cit.*

inner ego sees the imposing superiority. We see it as one born blind, who being healed sees the beauty of colours, or as one deaf, whose hearing being restored, catches the melodies from the world of sounds, and with his whole soul delights in them.[1]

Included among Rembrandt's best known works is his 'Portrait of an Old Woman' reading the Bible (1655) for which his mother sat as the subject. One of the most impressive features of the painting is the way in which the Bible she is reading appears to be the source of the light by which she is reading it. This wonderfully (and deliberately) captures the point. The Spirit does not *add to* Scripture in order to persuade us of its divine origin and character. Nor does he speak *apart from,* or even *alongside* Scripture to bring us to this persuasion. He speaks *through* the Scriptures themselves; he illumines its message by the message itself. We come to see the nature of Scripture in the light of Scripture itself.

John Calvin puts it like this: 'Scripture exhibits fully as clear evidence of its own truth as white and black things do of their color, or sweet and bitter things do of their taste.'[2]

This is what took place in the Acts of the Apostles, when the gospel spread beyond the bounds of the Jews.

The chancellor of Queen Candace of Ethiopia had travelled to Jerusalem to seek God. He came away, probably having managed to purchase a scroll of the prophecy of Isaiah. See him sitting in his swaying chariot, gripping the scroll to steady it as he reads in Isaiah 53 of a lamb who is led to the slaughter, and yet is wounded, bruised and chastised for the sins of others and, as a result, is highly exalted.

The description grips him. Yet it is also puzzling and mysterious. But then a voice beside the chariot enquires: 'Do you understand what you are reading?' It is Philip the evangelist. God has sent him to this seeker after truth. 'How can I understand', replies the Ethiopian, 'unless someone explains it to me?' Philip does, and the man becomes a Christian and is baptized. He is persuaded that the words on the scroll in his hand are the word of God.[3]

[1] A. Kuyper, *Encyclopaedia of Sacred Theology: Its Principles*, tr. J. H. de Vries (London: Hodder and Stoughton, 1899), p. 558.
[2] John Calvin, *Institutes* I.vii.2.
[3] *Acts* 8:26-40.

Sometimes God sends a Philip to those who are trying to understand his word. At other times he opens their hearts without any human agent. In either case the Spirit illumines our minds to see what is actually there and to recognise the voice that is speaking to us.

Many Christians, when asked how they became Christians, where they were when their hearts began to burn within them, or who helped them to begin to follow Christ, simply say: 'I was alone, reading the Bible, and it all began to fall into place. I understood, and I trusted. Once I was blind—the Bible was a closed book to me. Now I see.'

I had been reading the Bible for five years before I was able to say that. I started to read it as a primary schoolboy, thinking that reading the Bible and being a Christian were one and the same thing. Then, in my ordinary course of reading through John's Gospel I was arrested by these words: 'You search the Scriptures because you think that in them you have eternal life; and it is they that bear witness about me, yet you refuse to come to me that you may have life.'[1]

Suddenly it was clear. I had read the words before, but now I understood their meaning, and saw their implications. I too had been searching the Scriptures thinking that by so doing I would find eternal life. But I was looking at a book, not looking for Jesus. I had not come to him to find life!

Paul saw this happen on a large scale during his brief mission to Thessalonica. The Thessalonians recognised the voice of God speaking through his words.[2] It was a fulfilment of the promise of Jesus that when he called his sheep would recognise his voice and follow him.[3] It is always thus, whether on the road to Emmaus or in the city of Thessalonica in the first century, or to a young schoolboy in Glasgow. Or to monumentally significant figures like Augustine who, at the age of thirty-two, was delivered from the chains of his own sin and separation from God:

> I felt my past to have a grip on me. It uttered wretched cries: 'How long, how long is it to be?' 'Tomorrow, tomorrow?' 'Why not now? Why not an end to my impure life in this very hour?'

[1] *John* 5:39-40.
[2] *1 Thess.* 2:13.
[3] *John* 10:4, 16.

As I was saying this and weeping in the bitter agony of my heart, suddenly I heard a voice from the nearby house chanting as if it might be a boy or a girl (I do not know which), saying and repeating over and over again 'Pick up and read, pick up and read.' At once my countenance changed, and I began to think intently whether there might be some sort of children's game in which such a chant is used. But I could not remember having heard of one. I checked the flood of tears and stood up. I interpreted it solely as a divine command to me to open the book and read the first chapter I might find ... So I hurried back to the place where Alypius was sitting. There I had put down the book of the apostle when I got up. I seized it, opened it, and in silence read the first passage on which my eyes lit: 'Not in riots and drunken parties, not in eroticism and indecencies, not in strife and rivalry, but put on the Lord Jesus Christ and make no provision for the flesh in its lusts' (*Rom.* 13:13-14).

I neither wished nor needed to read further. At once, with the last words of this sentence, it was as if a light of relief from all anxiety flooded into my heart. All the shadows of doubt were dispelled ...

From there we went in to my mother, and told her. She was filled with joy. We told her how it had happened. She exulted, feeling it to be a triumph, and blessed you who 'are powerful to do more than we ask or think' (*Eph.* 3:20). She saw that you had granted her far more than she had long been praying for in her unhappy and tearful groans.[1]

There is coherence to this divine activity in which the Spirit-given word becomes the Spirit-illumined word. But it is not the logic of this world.

It is often argued that it is necessary to prove by rational argument that something is the case before it can be accepted as a starting place for further discussion or action.[2] But if the Bible is the word of God, what would be a sufficient proof that this was so? A lesser authority

---

[1] Augustine, *Confessions*, translated with an Introduction and Notes by Henry Chadwick (Oxford: Oxford University Press, 1991), pp. 152-153.

[2] Thankfully today many philosophers have come to acknowledge that there is no such thing as reasoning without a starting point (*e.g.*, that the process of reasoning is itself reasonable!).

cannot prove the authority of a greater. In this case 'only God is a fit witness to himself'.[1]

Thus the Spirit who gave the word in the first place is the one who also convinces us that this is what it is—the word of God.

There are many ways in which we can commend Scripture by life and lip, deed and word. We can explain the Bible's own claims; we can defend the Bible against attacks (even if C. H. Spurgeon said he would rather defend a lion!). But ultimately there needs to be an inner work of God in our hearts before we are really persuaded that the Bible is the living word of the living God, speaking to our deepest needs.

So, we believe the Bible to be God's word because its various contents express a conscious awareness of being God's word. In this sense Scripture presents itself to us as the word of God. As we read its pages and consider its message, the Holy Spirit convinces us through its teaching and its effect on us that this claim is the truth.

This explains why, when we find the reliability of the Bible under attack, and defend it in various ways, we have accomplished only part of what is necessary. For people become convinced of the authority of Scripture only by Scripture itself as the Holy Spirit persuades them that it is indeed the very word of God. Without this ministry sin-blinded eyes cannot see that Scripture is the word of God, sin-darkened hearts cannot respond to it as the word of God, and sin-deafened ears cannot hear the voice of the Father addressing them in it.[2] But when we hear God speaking, we are persuaded. For then the divine voice silences ours and finally persuades us that the Bible's claim is true. It is the word of God.

---

[1] The reference here is to words of the fourth-century theologian Hilary of Poitiers, *On the Trinity*, Book 1:18.

[2] Cf. the vivid and instructive use of the present tense in *Heb.* 12:5, where a quotation from *Prov.* 3:11-12 is prefaced by the words 'God is *addressing* you as sons.'

Part Two – Reading the Bible

4. Do-It-Yourself

THE invitation card to the meeting for young people announced the title of the talk: 'The Scarlet Cord'. I was intrigued.

The cord in question turned out to be the one given by the Israelite spies to Rahab, the lady of doubtful reputation who made her home in Jericho at the time of Joshua (*Josh.* 2:1-21; *Heb.* 11:31). She was to hang it from the window of her house (which was built into the city walls) as a sign to the invading forces. Their orders were to save those who lived in the house from which the cord was hanging (*Josh.* 6:15-25).

This much I already knew as the speaker introduced the theme of his talk. But his main message was this: the real meaning of Joshua chapters 2 and 6 is that the scarlet cord represents the blood of Christ shed for our sins on the cross. Only those who are protected by the blood of Christ can be saved.

Scarlet cord turns red

The talk stuck in my mind through my teenage years. Something about it niggled with me. How did the speaker get from the scarlet cord to the blood of Christ? Was the 'real meaning' of Joshua 2 actually a 'hidden meaning', a kind of code language (for 'scarlet' read 'red', for 'cord' read 'blood', for 'city walls of Jericho' read 'walls of the city of Jerusalem' and for 'hanging' read 'crucified')? Or was the scarlet cord no more and no less than … a cord that was easily seen because it was scarlet? Would it have made any difference if it had been a cord of a different colour?

Since the early years of the church many Christians have understood the 'real' meaning of Rahab's scarlet cord to be the message of the cross of Christ. Towards the end of the first century A.D., Clement of Rome wrote:

59

They [the spies] gave her a sign, namely that she should hang out of her house a scarlet cord, thus indicating that there would be redemption through the blood of the Lord for all those who believe and hope in God. You see, loved ones, there was not only faith, but prophecy in this woman. [1]

But was the scarlet cord a prophecy of the blood of Christ. Or was it just a scarlet cord?

Lame interpretation?

G. Campbell Morgan gives another illustration of the same approach to reading the Bible. He describes a particular preacher who

… preached on this text: 'So Mephibosheth dwelt in Jerusalem; for he did eat continually at the king's table; and was lame on both his feet.'
It is a beautiful story about David and his love for Jonathan. He (the preacher) made his divisions in this way:
'My brethren, we see here tonight, *first,* the doctrine of human depravity—Mephibosheth was lame. *Second,* the doctrine of total depravity—he was lame on both his feet. *Thirdly,* the doctrine of justification—he dwelt in Jerusalem. *Fourthly,* the doctrine of adoption—he sat at the king's table. *Fifthly,* the doctrine of the perseverance of the saints—he did eat at the king's table continually.'[2]

What are we to make of this approach to interpreting Scripture?

It certainly does not lack ingenuity! But that is part of the problem. In neither case do these interpretations explain the original meaning of the passage. Instead they see statements about historical events as symbols and codes containing either prophecies or doctrines. The 'meanings' suggested here do in fact express biblical truth, *but it is not the truth which these texts contain.* In reading Scripture this approach bypasses the basic meaning of the text for a 'higher' or 'hidden' meaning, usually one which teaches us about salvation.

The danger, of course, is that by applying such principles of interpretation we make the Bible say almost anything we want. We may

[1] *The First Epistle of Clement to the Corinthians,* Chapter XII, 7-8. Clement was a bishop (overseer) in the church in Rome around the close of the first century A.D.

[2] G. Campbell Morgan, *Preaching* (London: Hodder and Stoughton, 1937), pp. 115-116.

read into it what cannot be read out of it. To use more technical language, our interpretation will be *eisegesis* (reading into the text) rather than *exegesis* (reading out of the text what it actually says within both its narrower and broader contexts).

This may seem overly critical. But imagine yourself sitting in a group Bible study on 2 Samuel 9 (the passage in which Mephibosheth appears). The leader asks (as leaders often do): 'What does this passage say *to you*?'

Mrs Smith has been reading a book that suggested the interpretation above. 'Well, clearly, it's about how we are totally depraved in our sinfulness, but God justifies and adopts us. More than that, it teaches "once saved always saved" because the text says that "Mephibosheth ate *continually* from the king's table".'

Mr Jones then says, 'Are you sure this teaches *total* depravity ... after all, he was lame only in his legs. Surely that leaves room for a fair amount of free will in salvation?'

Mr White then pitches in: 'Yes! But surely "dwelling in Jerusalem" is more about the Christian abiding in Christ, not just about justification and adoption?'

Mrs White (who always sides with her husband, but usually goes one better!) now adds, 'Yes, that's right, Jim; but there's more—you see "dwelling in Jerusalem" and "eating at the king's table"—surely that's really a reference to the church and the Lord's Supper?'

Mr Clark, who doesn't speak often, or at any length, but always weighs his words carefully, then says, 'You know, I think this passage is just about the fact that Mephibosheth was actually lame in both feet. David showed faithfulness and kindness to him. Surely that shows us that the Spirit of the Lord was already at work in the Old Testament saints and they expressed what Paul calls "the fruit of the Spirit" in Galatians 5:22?'

The others look at him as though his reading of the passage seems far too obvious.

Mrs White chips in: '*Surely* there must be a *deeper* meaning than that?'

Mr Clark is a wise old Christian however, and says, 'Well, that's quite deep enough for me. I wish I showed more of the fruit of the Spirit like this! And, after all, isn't what the author actually wrote, guided by the Holy Spirit, quite deep enough for us?'

The cord in the story of Rahab? It was a cord. She was not saved because the cord was scarlet, or because it represented the blood of Christ, but because she placed her destiny in the hands of the covenant God of Abraham, Isaac and Jacob and threw in her lot with his covenant people. He is indeed the God who promised to send Christ and to bless the nations of the earth through the seed of Eve and Abraham. But had the cord been green, or even black, it would have made no difference to its 'meaning'. But because it is scarlet, by association of ideas it has come to be understood as symbolic of the blood of Christ. Colour association is, however, an unreliable principle of interpretation.

Similarly, we are not meant to see in Mephibosheth's double lameness a potted systematic theology, but to admire the care and mercy of God flowing through his servant David, and of the importance of remaining faithful to one's vows and promises. Ultimately that does lead us to Christ, David's greater Son. But we get to him by seeing this passage in its broader redemptive context, not by reading the passage as though it were a metaphor for something else.

I recall hearing of a Professor of Old Testament Studies who, in the course of a lecture on Exodus 38, asked his students what they thought was the 'meaning' of the various pegs or pins God commanded to be made for the tabernacle. His eager students sought to outdo each other in deep spiritual explanations. Eventually the shrewd Professor said, 'Ah, yes, of course. But could it just possibly be, gentlemen, that some of these tent pegs were there to hold up the tent?'!

Over the centuries, both in private and public interpretation of the Bible, this approach has been commonplace, and at times it has been dominant. Many Christians simply inherit it in the context in which they are spiritually nurtured. That is one reason it is so important for us to give some attention to how we approach understanding the Bible.

Paul laid down an important axiom for Timothy: 'Do your best to present yourself to God as one approved, a worker who has no need to be ashamed, rightly handling the word of truth.'[1] We are to *work* at Bible study. And therefore we need to learn to know how to interpret the Bible properly.

[1] *2 Tim.* 2:15.

Being workmen

The verb Paul used for 'do your best' (*spoudazein*) has the basic meaning 'to hurry'. It then came to express the idea of making a strenuous effort.[1] Here, as though to emphasise the energy that will be required, he suggests that Timothy's approach to Scripture should be that of a 'workman'. 'Rightly handling', sometimes unhelpfully translated 'dividing', is elsewhere used of building a road. Paul is therefore conveying a picture of strenuous effort being made in order to make a straight and reliable pathway into the Bible's message.

Handling the Bible properly can be hard work!

Alexander MacLaren, the famous Victorian minister, used to go into his study early each morning wearing heavy boots rather than soft slippers in order to remind himself that studying the word of God was hard work. There is an old adage: 'Half the bad theology in the world is due to suppressed perspiration.' It is the result of not really making the effort, taking the time, and exercising the necessary disciplines to try to grapple with what God is really saying in the pages of Scripture. (There are, of course, other reasons for the other half of 'bad theology'.)

The value of our Bible study depends on this. Are we willing to work at it? Sometimes Christians seem to suggest that if we find Bible study is hard work then we cannot be very spiritual. Perhaps that explains why so many people have been attracted to the more immediate, straight-from-heaven, no-need-to-study revelations that they claim have come to them in prophecies and tongues.

But the Scriptures do not disclose their riches to lazy minds and hearts. Paul urges Timothy *'Think over* what I say, for the Lord will give you understanding in everything.'[2] Christians need to *think* about what the Bible says.[3]

So, according to Paul, Bible study requires hard work ('a worker') and a correct approach ('rightly handling'), involving mental activity ('think'). That is why our forefathers used to speak about 'digging in' to Scripture.

If we are prepared for the hard work, the next stage is to learn to grow in our ability to read the Bible with understanding.

[1] Paul uses it in this sense in 2 *Tim.* 4:9, 21.

[2] 2 *Tim.* 2:7.

[3] For a brief valuable treatment of the importance of the mind in the Christian life see John R. W. Stott, *Your Mind Matters* (Leicester: Inter-Varsity Press, 1972).

Principles of interpretation

In this and the following three chapters we will look more fully at how to study the Bible. But before doing that we need some orientation.

One of the best brief statements on how to approach Bible study is found in *The Westminster Confession of Faith*:

> The whole counsel of God concerning all things necessary for His own glory, man's salvation, faith and life, is either expressly set down in Scripture, or by good and necessary consequence may be deduced from Scripture: unto which nothing at any time is to be added, whether by new revelations of the Spirit, or traditions of men. Nevertheless, we acknowledge the inward illumination of the Spirit of God to be necessary for the saving understanding of such things as are revealed in the Word: and that there are some circumstances concerning the worship of God, and government of the Church, common to human actions and societies, which are to be ordered by the light of nature, and Christian prudence, according to the general rules of the Word, which are always to be observed.

> All things in Scripture are not alike plain in themselves, nor alike clear unto all: yet those things which are necessary to be known, believed, and observed for salvation, are so clearly propounded, and opened in some place of Scripture or other, that not only the learned, but the unlearned, in a due use of the ordinary means, may attain unto a sufficient understanding of them.

> The infallible rule of interpretation of Scripture is the Scripture itself: and therefore, when there is a question about the true and full sense of any Scripture (which is not manifold, but one), it must be searched and known by other places that speak more clearly.[1]

Notice the big points here:

- All we need to know in order to love and glorify God is found in Scripture.

[1] *The Confession of Faith*, I:6, 7, 9.

• Although there are difficult sections in the Bible, all the basics of the Christian faith are clearly and simply stated or can be deduced from Scripture.

• We are in constant need of the Spirit's help to understand Scripture and apply it.[1]

• The way in which we come to understand the central teaching of Scripture is by disciplined use of the means God has given us to interpret it.

• When we read and apply Scripture we should read it in its own terms, and not impose on it what we think it should be saying.

• Each passage of Scripture has its own basic meaning within its context, not multiple possible (and equally valid) meanings.

Of course a passage may have various applications, and indeed apply in different ways to different contexts. In addition a statement may relate to something that takes place beyond the time period in which it was spoken or written, and thus may have both an immediate and a longer term function. But the Bible should not be read as though there were a surface meaning and a much more important meaning hidden within or lying underneath the text.[2]

Our basic approach to Bible study should be to read passages in their own context, and to understand them in the light of the rest of Scripture, remembering that all Scripture has the same ultimate source in the one true and living God.

Reading Scripture in its natural sense

So, first of all, Scripture is to be read and interpreted according to its natural sense. What does this mean?

---

[1] See 2 *Tim.* 2:17.

[2] The danger here is not limited to naive readers of Scripture. Scholars may fall into the same trap, and so weigh down their interpretation with technical data 'essential' for a right reading of the text, that one is left with the impression that both the authors and the first readers of the text would have felt themselves inadequate to understand it.

A passage of Scripture should be read in terms of the ordinary meaning of the words and statements it contains. 'The true and full sense of any Scripture ... is not manifold, but one'. We understand its meaning within both its immediate context in a book and its wider context within Scripture. The point is that passages do not have a series of special 'spiritual' meanings.

So called 'spiritual' interpretations have their roots partly in philosophies of antiquity with their radical antithesis between the material and this worldly (evil) on the one hand, and the heavenly and spiritual (good) on the other.[1] Interpretations of Scripture according to the natural sense of the passage were viewed as inferior to those which could relate everything to the immaterial world of the spirit. The result was the quest for hidden rather than plain meanings which could then give rise to application.

Already in Paul's day this way of thinking was influencing some Christians. For example, his words in 2 Thessalonians 2:2 seem to imply that some people had 'spiritualised' his teaching about the resurrection, and insisted that they had already experienced it.

Relatively early on in the history of the church it became commonplace to look for several meanings in any given passage of Scripture. These were often classified:

• The *literal* or *historical* meaning. This was what the passage said when understood by the ordinary rules of grammar.

• The *moral* (sometimes called the *tropological*) meaning—what did the passage have to teach about the practicalities of the Christian life? Here the *meaning* of the text tended to be extended and confused with its *application*.

• The *allegorical* meaning. An allegory is an extended narrative in which the details in the fictional world of the story represent events and experiences in the real world.[2]

[1] Hence Paul's words in *Col.* 2:8, 21-22.

[2] *The Pilgrim's Progress* is probably the best known allegory. In it the celestial city 'stands for' heaven; the city of destruction for this world; the burden on Christian's back represents the guilt of his sin, and so on. Allegories should be read as *allegories*. *Allegorical interpretation* misreads details in a narrative as though they were allegorical which the author did not intend to be understood allegorically.

• The *anagogical* meaning, which was closely related to the allegorical, but drew out the significance of the passage for the heavenly pilgrimage.

But if this approach was muddle-headed, how did its results sometimes give genuine practical help to Christians?

For two reasons. First, because these interpretations often expressed truth taught elsewhere in Scripture. But the overall long-term effect of this way of reading the Bible inevitably was to see meanings which simply did not exist in the text. Second, because even when the *interpretation* of the passage went awry it often dovetailed with an *application of the text* that was true.

The danger, however, is that when biblical truth is expressed, although not properly derived from the text under examination, no solid foundation undergirds it, thus undermining the biblical truth itself.[1]

Furthermore, there are no real controls in this system of interpretation.

So it cannot be over-stressed that the key to understanding Scripture is to understand it according to its *natural* sense. This means reading passages with sensitivity to their grammar and style, the kinds of genre of literature they illustrate, and their place within the grand narrative of the whole Bible.

Here it is helpful to distinguish between interpreting the Bible 'literally' (that is, taking the words and statements in their ordinary sense within their broader context) and what we might call 'literalistically' (that is, taking the words in a 'literal' sense irrespective of whether that sense is appropriate or not).[2]

---

[1] It is interesting, in this context, to notice how carefully leading Roman Catholic biblical scholars are at pains to point out that aspects of the church's teaching based traditionally on certain texts are not actually taught in those texts. At the same time they are careful to point out that they are not denying the truthfulness of the tradition, only the correctness of attributing it to certain biblical texts.

[2] *E.g.*, interpreting a statement made in poetry by reading it as if it were in prose, insisting that David was literally surrounded by bulls from Bashan, or that Paul must have fought with and Daniel-like subdued lions in Ephesus (*Psa.* 22:12; *1 Cor.* 15:32). Numbers of commentators have insisted in the case of Paul's words that he must have fought with non-human wild beasts. Perhaps he did, but in favour of the view that he is using a figure of speech here are: (1) that no reference to such

To understand the Bible literally, therefore, is not to insist that there are creatures of unimaginable features in heaven (as in the book of Revelation), but to recognise the intention of the writer and the kind of literature he was writing, and the overall purpose of the book he wrote. Revelation is a visionary (apocalyptic) book, filled with colourful and suggestive imagery. It is not an ordnance survey map of heaven, but a series of larger-than-life illustrations—sketches if you like—revealing the victory of Christ over all evil forces. Fail to understand this and we are likely to read Revelation as a puzzle to be solved rather than a vision given by Christ to encourage.

When we 'rightly handle the word of God' we no longer use it as a 'promise-box' in the hope that a single verse, or phrase, will leap out, hit us between the eyes, and get us through the day. Yes, God may impress a verse on our hearts and minds in order to help us. But he has given Scripture *as a whole* to us so that its entire message will become the framework of reference for the rest of our lives. We do not engage in Bible study in order to get a 'fix to last for today' but to learn how to think, feel, and act in a God-honouring way every day.

God wants us to grapple with the great truths of Scripture because they are life-long investments, not daily pick-me-ups. Our aim is to have an intimate acquaintance with the mind of God as he has revealed it in commands and promises, illustrated in and through the lives of biblical saints and in Jesus supremely. As we do so we will begin to discover—however slowly—what his will is in every situation and circumstance of life. We will have learned how to read and apply his word.[1]

This inevitably means *study.* There are things in the Bible that are difficult to understand.[2] There will be hard mental and spiritual work ahead of us as we grapple with its meaning. The student of the Bible

---

a remarkable event survives in Luke's account of his ministry at Ephesus; (2) the expression appears elsewhere metaphorically, not only in antiquity in general but also in the letter of Ignatius of Antioch to the Romans. To *insist* on the literal reading would be to go beyond the 'normal' use of the expression.

[1] Printed as Appendix B (see below, pp. 189-194), is an outstandingly helpful letter written by John Newton on the subject of Divine Guidance in which he has some wise words on applying the Scriptures.

[2] *2 Pet.* 3:16.

must be like a dog worrying a bone until he has managed to chew every last ounce of goodness out of it!

Years ago a friend confided in me that he was enjoying what he described as 'great Quiet Times' in his daily Bible reading and prayer. I asked him what part of the Bible he was reading through. He replied 'Ephesians'.

Having a suspicion that Christians often short-changed themselves in their daily Bible reading I asked: 'If I had given you a blank note-book at the beginning of the month, in which you had recorded your thoughts as you studied Ephesians each day, and you had returned it to me at the end of the month, what would I find in it? (a) An interesting narrative about your daily spiritual condition; or (b) A fairly clear outline of what Paul was actually saying to the Ephesians coupled with ways in which this teaching could be applied to your own life?'

His (anticipated!) answer was 'Oh, definitely (a)!'

I said, 'Why not give (b) a try now?'

He agreed to do so. The result, he later told me, transformed the value of his Bible study. Now—at the very least—he knew what Paul had written to the Ephesians. Beforehand all he could tell me was what he thought of his own spiritual condition! Now he had fuel for long-term meditation and application.

We do not grow as Christians merely by taking our spiritual temperature. Scripture teaches us that maturity comes from the life-transforming renewal of our minds.[1] That in turn comes from actually understanding and learning to apply God's word to our lives.

In order to do this well as Bible students we need to have some sense of the basic working principles of reading the Bible. To these we now turn in the next three chapters.

---

[1] *Rom.* 12:1-2.

5. Keys

G OD has spoken to us in his word. He has used our language, accommodating his thoughts to our capacity.

If you want to learn to play the piano, or to touch-type, you must first learn the keys, and practise until it becomes 'second nature' to you to use them properly. Similarly there are 'keys' in reading the Bible. Like musicians, some Bible readers grasp them intuitively. We simply know how to read—to a certain extent. But we want to be better readers, to understand more fully the message of Scripture. It is helpful, therefore, to know what to look for when we read the Bible.

In a sense this is simply stating the obvious. In order to understand any book we need to do this. Why emphasise it here in connection with the Bible?

We have already noticed that, precisely because it is the Bible—a unique God-breathed book—Christians sometimes read it as though it had not come to us through men. In addition, Scripture comes from a different time and culture from our own. We need to be sensitive to how this ancient literature works.

Musicians, artists, sportsmen develop great skills, yet always do so by going back to the basic principles. The same is true for us as Bible readers.

This chapter deals with five important keys.

Key 1: Context

The first step to understanding a passage is to read it in its own context. But what is reading Scripture 'in context'? It means reading each word as part of a sentence, each sentence within its paragraph, each paragraph within the chapter in which it appears, each chapter in its book, and each book in the context of its author's other writing, and then each author in the context of his place in God's on-going revelation so that ultimately we read a passage in the context of the whole biblical narrative.

Reading Scripture in context clarifies passages that may have puzzled us.

To take a well known example: many Christians reading and comparing Paul's words in Romans 3:28 ('We hold that one is justified by faith apart from works of the law') and James's words in James 2:24 ('You see that a person is justified by works and not by faith alone') have felt that these two passages contradict each other. Martin Luther's early conclusion was that this was certainly the case, and so he called the Letter of James 'a right strawy epistle'.

Had Luther been a little more patient he would have seen that these two passages only superficially contradict each other. In fact when we read each of them in its proper context they are in perfect harmony.

In Romans Paul stresses that salvation is by faith ('alone', as Luther insisted, *i.e.* not 'by works'). James however stresses that justifying faith is never 'alone'. Thus real faith never exists without bearing the fruit of a new obedience.

In fact the contexts of these two passages are a diameter apart.

Paul is dealing with what we might call 'legalism' (seeing human action as a ground for acceptance with God).

James, on the other hand, is dealing with the error of 'antinomianism' (if justification comes by faith then it doesn't matter how we live. Whether or not we do good works is irrelevant).

We learn from Paul that it is faith that saves, not human works. Yet elsewhere Paul teaches that this faith always shows itself by good works.[1] The faith that leads to justification by receiving Christ also leads to sanctification since justifying faith unites us to Christ. The person who is united to Christ in faith will always be a person who becomes obedient to Christ in love.

From James we learn that, like Abraham, we are justified by faith.[2] But Abraham-like faith that justifies necessarily expresses itself in the

---

[1] *E.g.*, *Eph.* 2:10. Note especially *Gal.* 5:6. See also *Rom.* 3:31.

[2] *James* 2:23. Both Paul and James see *Gen.* 15:6 as a key text ('Abraham believed God and it was counted to him as righteousness'). See *Rom.* 4:3.

obedient way Abraham's did. Accounted righteous by faith, he was counted as indeed righteous because he acted in obedience in being willing to offer up his son on Mount Moriah. God regarded him as a person in a right relationship with himself because his righteous actions demonstrated that he actually was![1] He was counted as a righteous person (someone in a right relationship with God) because his actions proved the reality of his faith.

Reading Scripture in context safeguards us against a concordance mentality

Understanding this simple principle—that words take their specific meaning from their particular context—preserves us from what we might call 'the concordance mentality' in which we imagine that the same word always means the same every time it appears.

The word 'flesh' serves as a good, and yet obvious example. Sometimes in Scripture it means simply our *physical* nature.[2] But at other times it refers to our *fallen* nature, the whole person under the dominion, and manifesting the effects, of sin.[3]

If we were to assume that every time the word 'flesh' appears in the Bible it always means the same thing, we would draw a deeply flawed conclusion, namely that the Bible regards physical existence ('flesh') as sinful in itself. That would then have an impact on our understanding of the words of John 1:14 that 'the Word became flesh', and would imply that Christ's human nature was sinful like ours.

Reading Scripture in context preserves us from 'the amplified mentality'

What is this? It is thinking that we can virtually choose any of the various meanings a dictionary may provide for a word. While words have a certain elasticity in meaning, ordinarily the context in which the word is used considerably narrows the particular nuance it will have in a given context.

It is here that a little knowledge of Hebrew or Greek can be a help or a hindrance. It is always helpful to be familiar with the language which lies behind a translation we use. But 'a little learning is a dangerous thing' if we take the misstep of randomly choosing one aspect

---

[1] *James* 2:22-26.
[2] As in 'flesh and blood', *Eph.* 2:15.
[3] As in *Eph.* 2:13.

of one dictionary meaning of the word without reference to its context.[1]

Application

When we read Scripture in context we not only understand it better, but we are also often better equipped to apply its teaching in a practical way. For the Bible is a fundamentally pastoral book, intended to lead us to the knowledge of God and obedience to his will. It is 'useful for teaching, rebuking, correcting and training'.[2] Patient reading and reflection on a passage within its context leads us to see how God's truth applied to the first readers serves as a bridge to the application of the same truth to our own lives.

Key 2: Jesus

An underlying theme in John's Gospel is that Jesus is 'on trial' before the watching world. Witnesses for the prosecution appear. But throughout the Gospel defence witnesses also appear (the woman at the well, the man born blind, Lazarus, and others[3]).

Jesus himself points out to his detractors that while, at the beginning of his ministry, John the Baptist bore witness to him, his own Father is his chief witness. They should have seen that in their Hebrew Bible (our Old Testament). It pointed to him, if only they had the eyes to see.

But, said Jesus, 'you do not have his word abiding in you ... You search the Scriptures because you think that in them you have eternal life; and it is they that bear witness about me, yet you refuse to come to me that you may have life.'[4]

Jesus is here chastising the Jewish leaders for their blindness to the central message of their Bible: 'they ... bear witness about me'. Ultimately the Bible is about God sending Jesus to be the Saviour.

[1] For an amusing illustration see General Sir John Hackett's autobiographical *I Was a Stranger* (London: Little Foxed, 1977), pp. 63-64. Seriously wounded in World War II, he was lovingly cared for by a Dutch family. One morning, he records, he was greeted 'gravely' by his host, *Dutch-English Dictionary in hand:* 'Good-day Mr Hackett. How is your *corpse?*'

[2] *2 Tim.* 3:16.

[3] *John* 4:1-42; 9:1-34; 11:1-12:11.

[4] *John* 5:39-40.

The significance of this becomes even clearer in Luke's description of Jesus' conversation with two disciples on the Emmaus Road on the afternoon of his resurrection: 'And beginning with Moses and all the Prophets, he interpreted to them in all the Scriptures the things concerning himself.'[1]

The Old Testament *as a whole* is a preparation for Jesus.[2] But Jesus must also have discussed particular passages with them to show how to connect the dots between the Old Testament and himself. The two disciples later described what had happened: Jesus 'opened to us the Scriptures'.[3]

Later that evening the whole group of disciples experienced something similar in Jerusalem. Pointing them to passages in 'the Law of Moses and the Prophets and the Psalms' Jesus 'opened their minds to understand the Scriptures'[4]—particularly as they related to his death and resurrection.

Paul picked up on this theme when he wrote to his young friend Timothy:

> But as for you, continue in what you have learned and have firmly believed, knowing from whom you learned it and how from childhood you have been acquainted with the sacred writings, which are able to make you wise for salvation through faith in Christ Jesus.[5]

Here, of course the expression 'the sacred writings' refers to the Old Testament Scriptures. Paul implies that they taught 'salvation through faith in Christ Jesus'.

The Lord Jesus is the centre of the Bible's message; he is the key to everything in it. So the questions we will always ask about a passage are: 'How is this connected to Jesus?' and 'How is Jesus connected to this passage?'

These connections will differ from passage to passage. But because of the unity of the Bible and because of its central theme of God

[1] *Luke* 24:27.
[2] A point vividly brought out in the two genealogies of Jesus (*Matt.* 1:1-17, tracing God's plan back to Abraham; Luke 4:23-38, tracing the grand narrative back to Adam).
[3] *Luke* 24:32.
[4] *Luke* 24:45.
[5] *2 Tim.* 3:14-15.

establishing his kingdom in Christ by the outworking of his covenant promise, they will always be there. There is a line that runs through the whole Bible from creation in Genesis 1 to re-creation in Revelation 22. Along that line we learn of man's sin, the fall, and his exile from Eden in Genesis 3 and of the grace, salvation, and the restoration and return to the garden through Christ which climaxes in Revelation 21-22.

Because the dominant plot line of the whole Bible is what God accomplishes through his Son, and in the power of the Spirit, from start to finish these sixty-six books tell a single, multifaceted story whose central character is Jesus Christ and what he does.[1] He is the one through whom all things were created,[2] in whom all things are held together,[3] and by whom God brings reconciliation.[4]

How we see the relationship of the Old Testament to Christ becomes clearer in the next key.

Key 3: The unfolding drama

There is a main plot in the dramatic story the Bible tells. And, of course, there are sub-plots within the plot. We might call these: 'The Grand Narrative', 'The Big Picture' and 'The Plot Line'.

The Grand Narrative begins in Genesis 1:1-2:3. God created the cosmos and placed man in a garden. In fact this garden is the 'temple' in which they were to live for God and worship him. Adam's task is described in language echoed in the later description of the priestly family's responsibilities in looking after the tabernacle.[5] Adam was to expand this garden-temple until it filled the whole earth.[6] Instead he fell and was 'excommunicated' from the Eden-temple.

The story that runs from Genesis 3 to Revelation 21-22 is about how the ruin Adam left will be restored by God into a final garden-temple. In the final garden-city there is no temple located in one particular

---

[1] I have attempted a brief summary of some ways in which the Old Testament narrative relates to Christ in *Preaching Christ from the Old Testament*, PT Media Paper # 2. This is currently available for download at: *http://www.old.proctrust.org. uk/dls/christ_paper.pdf.*

[2] *John* 1:1-3.

[3] *Col.* 1:16-17.

[4] *Col.* 1:20.

[5] *Gen.* 2:15. Cf. *Num.* 1:53; 3:8, 10, 32 and numerous other passages.

[6] *Gen.* 1:28.

location, 'for its temple is the Lord God the Almighty and the Lamb'.[1] In other words, all will be temple! God will accomplish in Christ what Adam was called to do, but failed to bring to pass.[2]

In order to bring this Grand Narrative to its conclusion, Scripture gives us a further focus.

The Big Picture begins in Genesis 3:15:

> The LORD God said to the serpent … 'I will put enmity between you and the woman, and between your offspring and her offspring; he shall bruise your head, and you shall bruise his heel.'

Within the Grand Narrative, we now discover how the drama will unfold. The curse God pronounces on the serpent will lead to ongoing conflict between two 'offspring'. It will climax in a final crisis in which one particular offspring of Eve will overcome the serpent himself.[3]

Notice the basic structure of this divine promise. There is:

Conflict:	between the serpent and the woman
Continuity:	between your offspring and her offspring
Climax:	between 'you' and 'he'

This leads us to:

The Plot Line. All this raises a question: How does God bring this

---

[1] *Rev.* 21:22.

[2] This is the clue to interpreting the otherwise perplexing statement by Paul in *I Cor.* 15:28 that when Christ has subjected everything to himself 'then the Son himself will also be subjected to him who put all things under him, that God may be all in all'. The context here underlines that Paul is speaking of the Son *in his role as the 'last Adam' and the 'second man'* (*I Cor.* 15:45, 47). He is 'last' because he accomplished what Adam failed to do and needs no successor; he is 'second' because there is no one between Adam and Christ capable of doing this. The Son took our human nature in order to accomplish this. The breathtaking vision of *I Cor.* 15:28 suggests that when Christ has restored all things, in his role as Last Adam, he will bring the glorified Eden and its citizens to the Father as the love-gift which Adam would have brought had he and we remained faithful and obedient.

[3] That the ongoing conflict leads to an *individual* denouement seems to be implied by the fact that the promise moves from a corporate conflict on both sides (seed of woman, seed of serpent) to an individual (serpent) implying that a similar movement from corporate to individual is also true on the side of the seed of the woman.

to pass? The biblical answer is two dimensional: He establishes his kingdom of grace by fulfilling the promises of his covenant. So, when we read the Big Picture as it unfolds in a series of shorter stories, we need to do the following:

- Keep an eye on the plot line.

- Ask: What is happening to the (covenant) promise as God keeps his word and establishes his kingdom, or as his people rebel against him and experience covenant judgment?

- Read each narrative in the light of the ongoing conflict promised in Genesis 3:15.

- Understand that those involved in the advance of the plot line will, to some degree or another, have their lives drawn into the pattern by which God will ultimately fulfil his promise in the sufferings, death, resurrection, and triumph of the Lord Jesus.

The familiar Old Testament narrative of the life of Joseph in Genesis 37-50 illustrates how this works. What a story! But, notice:

This is not simply an isolated, albeit marvellous, boys' adventure story. It is part of a larger plot. The larger context is the way God keeps his covenant with Abraham. He had promised that this would involve his people becoming slaves in Egypt before being delivered by his hand.[1]

This covenant context is further underlined by the fact that the Joseph narrative is actually part of the larger story of Jacob's family.[2] God is the God of Abraham, Isaac, and Jacob—the truth that God later stresses to Moses when the covenant promise of the Exodus is about to be kept.[3]

The narrative is full of tension. God's promise is certain, but it often seems fragile. Joseph's experiences, while individual and personal, also fit into a much larger picture. The brothers' jealousy and hatred, Potiphar's wife's sin, the cupbearer's forgetfulness, are all part of the ongoing conflict between the kingdom of darkness and the kingdom

---

[1] *Gen.* 15:12-16.
[2] As *Gen.* 37:1-2 indicates.
[3] *Exod.* 3:6; 6:8.

of God. On these three occasions it seems as though God's covenant promise and purpose will fail.

Throughout the narrative Joseph's life illustrates a pattern that reaches its fulfilment in the life, suffering, death, resurrection, ascension, and enthronement of the Lord Jesus at the right hand of God to be our Prince and Saviour. Hence his last recorded words in Genesis 50:20.

That pattern is seen later in the New Testament as the fruit of faith that brings us into union and communion with Christ. We share in his death, resurrection, and ascension.[1] But even before his coming, through faith in the promised Saviour, Joseph's life shares this same pattern. The death and resurrection of Christ cast their shadow backwards into the lives of believers in the promise in the days of the old covenant as well as forwards into the lives of members of the new covenant community today.

We find similar dynamics in an even more obvious way in the story of David and Goliath. Again, what a story! But it is not simply a story about how little people can stand up to (and beat up!) big people. The narrative is part of the larger drama in which the kingdom of darkness is seeking to destroy the covenant promise of God by placing the people of God under threat of subjugation if not actual extinction. Here again we see prefigurings of the pattern God uses in the ultimate salvation of his people: 'God chose what is foolish in the world to shame the wise; God chose what is weak in the world to shame the strong.'[2] All this is then part of a larger story in which David discovers that trusting in God's covenant promise involves him 'sharing in advance' in the sufferings and triumph of the ultimate King who would fulfil the promise of kingdom restoration. This, of course, comes to vivid expression in many of the psalms.[3]

Joining the dots

Parents give their children puzzle books to keep them amused on long journeys. Frequently these books contain 'Join the Dots' pictures. Adults often see the picture simply by looking at the dots. But our

---

[1] *Rom.* 6:1 ff; *Gal.* 2:20; *Phil.* 3:10-12; *Col.* 2:9-3:17.
[2] *1 Cor.* 1:27.
[3] *E.g., Psa.* 2; 22; 23; 69; 110.

children need to trace the lines indicated by numbers to complete the picture and tell us what it is.

As the Grand Narrative of Scripture unfolds it contains 'dots' that we need to 'join up' in order to see how God establishes his kingdom in Christ, in fulfilment of the promise of Genesis 3:15. The line it encourages us to trace takes us through a series of further promises or covenants. It is not difficult to 'join up the dots' in this story:

In advancing his purposes expressed in his (covenant) promise to Adam—[1]

God makes a covenant with Noah and his family.[2] Because he is going to send the Deliverer, despite the waywardness, sin, and rebellion of man, he will preserve the world from final judgment. Indeed, he is willing to begin again, as it were, with Noah who is given the same command Adam first received.[3]

God then calls Abram out of his pagan environment and makes his covenant with him and his offspring. In due season the nations of the world will be blessed through him.[4] This is the promise Paul would later see fulfilled in Jesus.[5]

When the immediate aspects of the covenant with Abraham had been fulfilled and the people were set free in the Exodus,[6] God made a further covenant, this time with Moses and the people.[7] This covenant was a comprehensive covenant, detailing the blessings God would pour out on his faithful people (and the judgment curses they would experience if they lived as the seed of the serpent rather than the seed of faith). It also contained a detailed pattern for their lifestyle.

This is the covenant the New Testament refers to as 'the old covenant'. The key to understanding it is to recognise that its provisions were always intended to form an interim covenant, not the final one. They were to function so long as God's people all belonged to a single nation. When God's kingdom became 'international' on the day of

---

[1] *Gen.* 3:15. In fact the 'promise' to Adam and Eve is 'overheard' from the threatened curse on the serpent.

[2] *Gen.* 8:9.

[3] Cf. *Gen.* 9:1 with *Gen.* 1:28.

[4] *Gen.* 12:1-3; 15:1-21; 17:1-14.

[5] *Gal.* 3:16.

[6] *Gen.* 15:12-16.

[7] *Exod.* 6:2-5; 19:5.

Pentecost, those local-and-interim provisions came to an end. Thus, for example, the provisions about sacrifices, and the food laws, and the way in which the calendar was regulated, were intended only for the period between Moses and Jesus.

God's 'moral law' is, however, a constant. The Ten Commandments transpose into the lifestyle of man, God's image, the character of God himself. In the Decalogue this is expressed in a form suited to his sinful people between the time of Moses and the coming of Christ. Thus the Ten Commandments are expressed largely in a negative form. We all express family rules negatively for our children when they are young. It is easier for the children with wayward tendencies to grasp 'Don't stick the screwdriver into the electric socket' than to explain to them how electricity works and why it can kill them. That follows in due course. Similarly for his under-age and wayward-tending children God gave ten basic life commandments largely in a negative form.[1] In addition he provided applications of them appropriate to the period between Moses and Jesus in which his purposes were being worked out specifically through one nation. Of course, as Jesus made clear, the *negative* expressions in the Ten Commandments always implied heart-searching positive commands which Christians are to fulfil through the power of the Holy Spirit as the image of God is restored.[2]

Within the context of the covenant with Moses, God then made a covenant with David.[3] Now it was becoming clearer that the Messianic King who would deliver his people was not only the seed of the woman, and the seed of Abraham, but specifically would come from the family line of David.

All these 'new' covenants and their promises then pointed forward to the 'new covenant' which Jeremiah described,[4] and which Jesus himself announced was fulfilled in him.[5] God's covenant promises were fulfilled not by the sacrifice of animals on the altar in Jerusalem, but by the sacrifice of his Son, the Lord Jesus, on the cross of Calvary. In him all the Old Testament's pictures of the Redeemer are united. He is

[1] *Exod.* 20:3, 4, 7, *Job*, 13, 14, 15, 16, 17.
[2] See *Matt.* 5:17-48; *Rom.* 8:3-4; *Eph.* 4:24; *Col.* 3:9-10; *Rom.* 8:29.
[3] *2 Sam.* 23:5.
[4] *Jer.* 31:31-34. Cf. *Isa.* 42:6; 49:8.
[5] *Luke* 22:20.

the seed of the woman;[1] the priest like Melchizedek,[2] the prophet like Moses,[3] the king from David's line,[4] the son of man seen in Daniel's vision,[5] and the suffering servant described by Isaiah.[6] Christ himself is the new covenant.[7]

Key 4: Biblical logic

There is also an important logic enshrined in Scripture which helps us grasp the shape of God's work both for us and in us.

God works graciously for men, and *on that basis* he summons them to faith and obedience. In grammatical terms, biblical *imperatives* ('Do this') are always based on and resourced by biblical *indicatives* ('I the Lord have done this for you').

This logic was already present in creation:

Indicative: I have given you every good gift to enjoy, and a garden to care for and to enlarge

Imperative: Therefore exercise your dominion, and show you love me by not eating of the fruit of the tree of the knowledge of good and evil.

It is later present in the giving of the law:

Indicative: (a) Identity: I am the LORD your God
(b) Activity: who brought you out of the land of Egypt

Imperative: (1) You shall have no other gods before me
(2) You shall not ...

Recognising that this is the biblical pattern is essential if we are to understand how the message of the Bible (and therefore the Bible itself) works.

[1] *Gen.* 3:15. See *Rev.* 12:1-6.
[2] *Psa.* 110:1, 4. See *Heb.* 5:5-6.
[3] *Deut.* 18:15. See *Acts* 3:22-24.
[4] *2 Sam.* 7:16. See *Matt.* 1:6, 16.
[5] *Dan.* 7:13-22. See *Matt.* 16:13-16.
[6] *Isa.* 52:13-53:12. See *John* 12:38.
[7] See *Isa.* 42:6; 49:8; *Jer.* 31:31; *Luke* 22:20; *1 Cor.* 11:25.

For one thing it is a major key to the unity of the Bible. Understand this and we will not fall into the common trap of thinking that salvation in the old covenant was by works while in the new covenant it is by grace. It was always by grace. Always God's indicatives preceded and undergirded his imperatives. This is why the apostles could appeal to the Old Testament to illustrate and vindicate the gospel of grace they preached and about which they wrote. Nor will we make the old error of thinking that the God of the Old Testament is severe and unyielding while the God of the New Testament is warm and friendly. This is both obvious and important when we read the New Testament. Always God's work logically precedes man's response and is the basis for it. Always grace precedes gratitude. Always, as a direct consequence, doctrine undergirds application in the teaching of the apostles.[1]

This pattern is particularly clear in Paul's letters to the Romans and to the Ephesians. The 'practical' sections of these letters are simply the flowering of the doctrinal sections from which they have emerged. Profound doctrinal teaching provides the foundation for wide-ranging ethical and spiritual application. Indeed it is the depth of the grace expounded that makes it safe for Paul to issue his vigorous and all-demanding imperatives without causing his readers to despair. The richer the grace the more rigorous the commands it is able to sustain.

The doctrinal teaching also shapes the ethical teaching. The emphasis is: because God is this and has done that (followed by the explanation of some truth), you should behave like this (followed by the exposition of how the Christian is to live). Understanding these patterns—having an outline in our minds of the general direction in which a writer is heading, and how he is dividing his material—helps us to handle God's word with the care and reverence which it merits.

Reading Scripture in context also means that we need to be sensitive to the kind of literature we are reading (its genre). Poetry is not prose; parables are not historical narratives. Key five, therefore is:

---

[1] Even when a command precedes a statement about God's provision in the order of writing, in biblical logic it is based on God's provision in the order of the gospel.

Key 5: Each part of Scripture should be read according to its literary character

We must always bear in mind the kind of literature we are reading. We do not read Revelation in the same way we read Chronicles. If we did, and read the book of Revelation as though it were history written in advance, we would misunderstand its message. In all likelihood we would build teaching on it that would not be consistent with the rest of Scripture. Revelation is a picture book, not a puzzle book containing a hidden outline of future world history.

But this point—understanding how to read different kinds of genre—is a topic all on its own, and to it we must turn our attention in the next chapters.

6. Prose, Poetry, Wisdom, and Prophecy

THE Bible (Greek: *biblos* = book) is in fact a book of books. It contains sixty-six books in total, thirty-nine in the Old Testament and twenty-seven in the New Testament. The Hebrew Bible (our Old Testament) contained the same books but arranged them in twenty-four books, counting as one book each Samuel, Kings, Chronicles, and Ezra-Nehemiah and the twelve so-called Minor Prophets. As we have seen, these were 'catalogued' in a threefold division: the Law, the Prophets, and the Writings:

The Law (*Torah*) was composed of the first five books of the Old Testament often called the Pentateuch (Genesis to Deuteronomy). *Torah* is the Hebrew word for 'instruction' and is a much broader concept than our term 'law'. This explains why the law we find in the Bible has the atmosphere of 'The Maker's Instructions'. Seeing it this way guards us against the danger—which lies at the heart of both legalism and antinomianism—of separating the laws of God from the person of God. God's *torah* is his gracious and wise direction to his people to enable them to live in fellowship with him. It has a personal, rather than a clinical spirit.

The Prophets were divided into two groups:
(1) The Former Prophets: Joshua, Judges, Samuel, Kings
(2) The Latter Prophets: Isaiah, Jeremiah, Ezekiel plus 'The Book of the Twelve Prophets' (Hosea to Malachi, known as 'The Minor Prophets', not because they were younger or unimportant but because these books are much briefer than the others).

The *Former* Prophets recorded events in the history of Israel and interpreted them in the light of the exposition of the covenant contained in Deuteronomy.

The *Latter* Prophets contain records of the proclamation and application of the implications of this same covenant and anticipate ways in which it would unfold in the future.

The Writings were composed of all the other books and were subdivided into three groups:

(1) Psalms, Proverbs, Job

(2) 'The Five Scrolls': Song of Solomon, Ruth, Esther, Lamentations, Ecclesiastes

(3) Daniel, Ezra-Nehemiah, Chronicles

Literary genre

The Bible contains not only different books, but different kinds of literature (often called 'genre'). These 'work' differently. Every genre has its own style and way of using language.

When a book opens with the words 'Once upon a time …', you know you are reading a 'fairy story' or a fantasy. Consequently you do not read it as if it were a history book.

If it begins, 'It was 29600 and the Megates ruled the Fourth Dimension' you know that you are reading science fiction, and you adjust to a sympathetic reading of life in another time, place, and dimension from our own.

But if a book begins with the words, 'All Gaul is divided into three parts' then, as every schoolboy used to know, you are reading Julius Caesar's *The Gallic Wars*—an historical account from a personal perspective.

The mention of the term 'genre' may evoke the reaction, 'Please, not another lecture on how I need to become a literary expert before I can read my Bible!' Understandably so, because it is just at this point that it becomes tempting for scholars to refer to the importance of 'hermeneutics' and to drown readers under a tsunami of technical information about how literature works, how language functions, how important various parts and figures of speech are, and how by doing prescribed exercises we will eventually be able rightly to read the Bible.

Lectures in hermeneutics—the science of interpretation—have their place. But this is not it. God has spoken in order to be understood by ordinary people such as ourselves. Most of us learned to read a long time ago, have been doing it for most of our lives, and are actually capable of reading and enjoying books! In the wise words of *The Westminster Confession*:

> those things which are necessary to be known, believed, and observed, for salvation, are so clearly propounded, and opened in some place of Scripture or other, that not only the learned, but the unlearned, in a due use of the ordinary means, may attain unto a sufficient understanding of them.[1]

We should not despair of our ability to read the Bible because we are unfamiliar with the laws of language. Most readers of the Bible throughout history—and perhaps most of the authors!—shared that unfamiliarity. After all, we use language every day.

Having said this, however, it is also true that we can become better, more informed, even more mature readers of Scripture. What most of us need is encouragement, and road signs on the way that will enable us to see what we otherwise might miss in Scripture. We then learn to read better *as we read.*

Eventually it may prove very helpful to read one of the many books on studying and interpreting the Scriptures.[2] But in fact most, if not all, of the authors of such manuals developed their reading skills slowly and gradually by ... *reading.* Lessons in grammar, exegesis, hermeneutics came later. They helped fine-tune reading skills, corrected some errors, and stimulated more penetrating and analytical reflection.

So what follows in this chapter and the next assumes that what most of us need is a few basic principles that will help us to make progress *as we read.*

In this chapter we will look at the Old Testament and reflect on Narrative, Poetry, Wisdom Literature, and Prophecy. In the next chapter we will focus on the New Testament and consider Gospels, Epistles, and Apocalyptic (the book of Revelation).

Narrative

About forty per cent of the Old Testament is in the form of narrative. In broad terms this includes all the books from Genesis to Esther. Of

---

[1] *The Confession of Faith*, I.7.
[2] A few suggested books are included in the Bibliography for Further Reading in Appendix C, see below, pp. 195-196.

course narrative is also woven into the Prophets, and the books of Job and Daniel.

Narrative would seem to be the easiest genre for us to read. We all love stories. But it can be very helpful to articulate for ourselves how biblical stories function.

As with all parts of Scripture we need to learn to set each book, each extended plot, and each part of the plot, within its various contexts— The Grand Narrative, the Big Story, and the Plot Line.

Narratives tend to follow a general set pattern with several typical elements:

(1) A setting in history, which gives rise to

(2) A specific situation, in which

(3) A problem or crisis arises, leading to

(4) A turning point in the drama, which then brings it to

(5) A resolution.

The plot line may not be quite as straightforward as this; and the resolution may simply be an interim one which then becomes the setting in history for a further development of the plot.

A good illustration of this is found in the little book of Ruth. It is a useful primer because the entire narrative is virtually self-contained in four chapters. In chapter 8 we will examine it in a more detailed fashion. But here notice how the drama is worked out.

The general stages are:

• *Setting:* 1:1. The action takes place in the days of the Judges. Individualism is rife.[1]

• *Situation:* 1:2. Elimelech of Bethlehem, his wife Naomi and their two boys leave the promised land because of famine and go to Moab.

• *Problem:* 1:3-5. Elimelech dies, the boys marry into (pagan) Moabite families, and then they in turn die. Naomi is husbandless and childless, bereft of love, care and provision.

• *Turning Point:* 1:6-18. Naomi decides to return home. The famine is over. Her daughters-in-law plan to accompany her. Naomi urges them to stay because their prospects in Bethlehem will be non-existent. One of the daughters-in-law, Orpah, returns home. The other,

[1] *Judg.* 21:25.

Ruth, insists on accompanying her, because Naomi's God and people have become hers also.

• *Resolution:* 1:19-22. The two women return and are greeted by the people of Bethlehem, Naomi acknowledges the sovereign hand of the Lord in her 'bitter' experiences.

But rather than being the end of the story, this is simply one narrative within the larger plot in chapters 2-4:

• *Resolution now becomes setting:* The two women return to Bethlehem at barley harvest—a hint that the story will develop around a harvest theme.

• *Problem:* Naomi and Ruth appear to be without resources; but God has established a law of 'gleaning'[1] from which they benefit. We are being encouraged as readers to wonder: Is God's legal provision in the past a hint that he will provide in the present and future for these two women?

• *Turning Point:* Ruth 'happened' (2:3) to find herself gleaning in the field of a godly man called Boaz. He shows her great kindness (which in the Old Testament is one of the chief characteristics of the Lord himself). Thus a hint is given to the reader: Keep your eye on Boaz.

Naomi realises that Boaz is actually a relative (2:20). She now thinks about another law God had established. The Levirate and Kinsman-Redeemer Laws placed responsibility to help in a time of family need on the wider family. Will this be the solution to the problem?

Now Naomi hatches a 'marry me' plot (3:1-5). Can Boaz be 'the answer' to an anxious (but meddling) Naomi? God has shown kindness; so has Boaz. Will God now show more kindness *through* Boaz?

• *Resolution:* In kindness Boaz handles a very delicate situation[2] with deep integrity. Not only so, but he showers kindness on the two women. He gives Ruth six measures of barley, which would raise a smile for the first readers and hearers–Ruth was carrying home perhaps

---

[1] *Deut.* 24:19.

[2] It would be a rash interpreter who thought that sending a widowed daughter-in-law to lie down at a man's feet in the middle of the night was any wiser in the days of the Judges than it would be in the twenty-first century!

seventy pounds in weight. Boaz had to 'put it on her'.[1] He will take care of things. Will this mean marriage to Ruth? The suspense builds.

• *Resolution now becomes setting again:* Chapter 4 describes how Boaz intends to pursue his commitment to marry Ruth.

• *Problem:* We now discover that there is someone with a stronger family claim to help Naomi (3:12).

• *Turning Point:* Boaz righteously invites the closer relative to discuss things with the city fathers (4:1-2). He shrewdly approaches the issue along the lines of the purchase of a field that belonged to Elimelech's family. When the man says he will 'do the right thing' and buy the field, Boaz then tells him there is a second part to the deal; a young widow!

• *Resolution:* Boaz has assessed the situation correctly. The man has too much to lose if he marries Ruth. The closer relative blurts out: 'Then you buy the field', with the implication, 'and you take the woman!'

The way is now clear. Boaz and Ruth marry. They have a son. Naomi and her late husband Elimelech now have an heir.

• *The Grand Narrative:* In this context God shows his covenant faithfulness. The family turns its back on his promises, and leaves the covenanted land rather than trust him. But leaving the promised land leads to death and barrenness. Naomi returns to the promised land (significantly, the verb 'return' is also used in the Old Testament for 'repent'). Whereas covenant disloyalty led to grief, covenant faithfulness leads Naomi back into the blessing of God. The road is rough, but the Lord is kind: he restores, he supplies.

But remember that there is

The Big Picture: This story is part of the Abrahamic covenant promise that in the seed of the woman 'all the families of the earth' would be blessed.[2] Ruth comes from one of those 'families'. She is a Gentile, from outside of the nation of Israel. Already God is keeping his promise.

---

[1] *Ruth* 3:15.
[2] *Gen.* 12:3.

The Plot Line: The book ends with a family tree.[1] Only in the closing words do we discover the bigger story of which this family narrative is a significant part: Naomi, Ruth, and Boaz are all part of the family tree that runs through Jesse to King David.[2]

Brilliant!

Thus only in the final word of the book ('David') do we discover what it is really all about: this is how God is unfolding his covenant promise to Abraham. This is not simply Ruth's story, it is Abraham's story. And it is also David's story.

But as we shall see in chapter 8, we know even more than the author. For when we set these details within the context of the whole story of redemption this family tree is seen to have epoch-making significance.

Large sections of the Old Testament (and indeed the New) are in this narrative form. But the Old Testament has other genres.

Poetry

Much of the Old Testament is written in the form of poetry. Modern translations make this clear visually by the way they set the text. There are also flashes of poetry embedded in the historical narratives, in the Prophets and in the Writings. But when we think of poetry in the Bible we inevitably think first of all about the Psalms.

The Psalms constituted the praise and prayer book of the Old Testament church. They can be divided into several categories, or sub-genre: there are songs of praise, confessions of sin, laments, meditations on the believer's relationship to God, the world, God's providences, as well as psalms for specific occasions. Each of these life-contexts influences the style and atmosphere of the psalm.

Psalms also address different 'hearers':—

- sometimes the hearer is the psalmist himself (*e.g. Psa.* 42; 43);
- sometimes, however, the hearer is intended to be others (*e.g. Psa.* 50);
- sometimes the hearer is the Lord alone (*e.g. Psa.* 51).

---

[1] *Ruth* 4:18-22.
[2] *Ruth* 4:22.

Poetry in motion

We think of rhythm, rhyme, and a particular way of using language as the chief characteristics of poetry written in the English language. Hebrew poetry also employs rhythm and poetic language. But in addition it exhibits a less familiar feature called 'parallelism'.

Parallelism has different forms, but its essence is the use of two or even three lines to describe aspects of the same reality, helping us see the whole picture as it were. It appears in different forms:

• *Repetition:* line two says more or less the same as line one but in different words. Together the two lines express the one idea more fully (synonymous parallelism).

• *Addition:* line one is true, but there is something more than this now expressed in line two (synthetic parallelism).

• *Contrast:* line one is true, but we need to be aware of a very different consideration expressed in line two (antithetical parallelism).

We find this also in Proverbs.

A further development of this pattern may appear in an entire psalm or section of Scripture where the second half of the passage seems to reverse, and even answer the order of what is said in the first part. This is what is known as chiasm (from the Greek letter *chi*—χ). This pattern not only gives a certain aesthetic pleasure, but on a larger scale it may also help us to detect the shape of the underlying story. We are not simply being told that one thing follows another but that a reversal, a divine answer and restoration are all taking place in the narrative.

Poetic language

English poetry abounds in the non-literal use of language. Hebrew poetry similarly employs figures of speech to describe actual experiences. We usually recognise this intuitively. But it is always worth bringing it to the forefront of our minds as we read.

Thus, in Psalm 22 the psalmist writes:

> Many bulls encompass me;   (a)
> Strong bulls of Bashan surround me[1]   (b)

---

[1] *Psa.* 22:12.

There is *parallelism*: line (b) is telling us that line (a) is true, but there is more: not only do the bulls surround him; these bulls are 'strong' and from 'Bashan'.

There is also *poetic language*. The 'bulls' here are not four-legged animals but violent opponents. Later in the psalm, he will use more animal analogies, describing his enemies as lions and dogs.[1] He is thus describing his experience so that we can intellectually 'understand' and also emotionally 'feel' the extremity of his situation. The poetic language thus heightens our mental perception, and draws us into the reality of his situation in a way that saying 'I was surrounded by my enemies' would not. This is but one of the many ways in which the literature of Scripture speaks to the whole person.

Spiritualising?

Earlier we stressed that we ought not to 'spiritualise' when we are interpreting Scripture. Now we are saying that sometimes language is used in 'poetic' ways in Scripture. Is this not 'spiritualising'? No. For the point being made earlier was that spiritualising reads the text in a way that is different from the author's intention. But when a writer uses language poetically, he means it to be interpreted figuratively rather than literally. Here we are reading the text in the way the author intended.

Turning point

Many psalms have a similar narrative 'shape'. They are like a parabola (a 'U'-shape).[2] It might be like this:

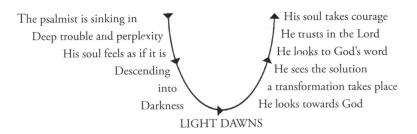

The psalmist is sinking in
Deep trouble and perplexity
His soul feels as if it is
Descending
into
Darkness

His soul takes courage
He trusts in the Lord
He looks to God's word
He sees the solution
a transformation takes place
He looks towards God

LIGHT DAWNS

[1] *Psa.* 22:13, 16, 21.
[2] Well described by Walter Brueggemann as 'disorientation' and 'reorientation'. W. Brueggemann, *The Message of the Psalms* (Minneapolis: Augsburg, 1984), pp. 9 ff.

Psalm 102 illustrates this 'shape':—

Verses 1-11: The author is overwhelmed by his situation. He shows many signs of depression: he feels horribly alone, he cries almost constantly, he is off his food, he feels everyone despises him; he even feels God has treated him like a plaything. He is near rock bottom: 'I wither away like grass.'[1]

But then something remarkable happens. He turns a corner.

Verses 12-22: His gaze is diverted for a moment from himself (*'my'*, *'I'*, *'my'*, *'I'*, *'I'* ...) and he sees the Lord in his eternal power, perfect goodness, amazing kindness (*But you, O LORD, are enthroned ...*').

Verses 23-24: Without any apparent explanation he is discouraged again. After taking two steps forward he appears to take one step back. But it is only *one* step. He has not sunk down as far as he had in verses 1-11. Progress has been made.

Verses 25-26: He rises again. Now he is a man convinced of God's unchanging character—precisely what he had doubted in verse 10. Now he sees God as the bedrock reality for his life.

Thus the man who in verse 4 described his days as smoke and his life as desperately lonely in verse 6, experiencing sleepless nights in verse 7, engulfed with grief in verse 9, is, by the close of the psalm in verse 28 now thinking about how God will bless his children and grandchildren!

As we follow this pattern we can hardly avoid seeing applications: (1) Believers too may be deeply distressed and depressed. (2) Believers at times may misunderstand both what God is doing (or not doing) and his character; (3) Believers need to have their understanding and emotions recalibrated by the truth about God; (4) Spiritual recovery may not be a straight line graph of unbroken progress; (5) Restoration has taken place when the truth transforms our perspective and our attitude.

True and false?

As we grow in our reading sensitivity we may occasionally notice that an individual's description of his experience may err.

---

[1] *Psa.* 102:11.

Errors in the infallible Scriptures? A moment's reflection will reassure us that this is not an embarrassment to those who believe the Bible is the word of God. Scripture is God-breathed and as such it is infallible. It is without error. But that includes recording lies and mistaken interpretations of God's character and providences when they occur within the narrative. Thus Genesis 3 contains a reliable-infallible account of the lies of the serpent by which Eve was deceived (her own words[1]).

This should not disturb us. Neither Satan nor his words are trustworthy or infallible. He is a liar and murderer from the beginning said Jesus.[2] We should expect that he would lie. What God gives us in Scripture is a trustworthy account of his lies.

The biblical record, then, does not fail us. But we would fail it if we misread the text and did not detect any lie it contained. This is obvious in Genesis 3. It may be less obvious, however, when Scripture is recording error in understanding God and his ways.

The book of Job as a whole provides us with an example. As readers we are given access in the first two chapters of the book to what lies behind the drama of the catastrophic tragedies Job experiences. But neither Job nor any of his famous 'comforters' has that access. They are like men trying to open a locked door in the dark by using the wrong key.

Occasionally Job seems almost to grasp the truth. Thus, in the midst of describing what he interprets as God's attacks on him he asks: 'If it is not he, who then is it?'[3] If this were a drama performed in the theatre the audience would be caught up in the tense emotions of the moment, and be on their feet and shouting: 'Job, it's not God! We know what's happening to you. It isn't God, Job. It's Satan who is at work to destroy you and your faith!' But Job gets only to the verge of understanding that the hand that is against him is not—despite his friends' claims—the hand of God. No, it is the hand of Job's and God's enemy.

In addition Job's friends utter some of the most magnificent statements about God anywhere to be found in the Bible. But they too are

[1] *Gen.* 3:13, reflecting on *Gen.* 3:1-7.
[2] *John* 8:44.
[3] *Job* 16:24.

living in a two-dimensional world. They distort the truth by saying
that he is suffering because he has sinned against the glorious God
they describe. But we know from the prologue that the truth is actually the reverse—Job is suffering because he is faithful to this God![1]

Something similar can be seen in Psalm 102. The psalmist, as we
have seen, is in great dejection of spirit. There were several reasons
for this. National affairs were at a low ebb—he speaks of the stones
and dust of Jerusalem, and is longing for the day when she would be
rebuilt.[2] He is deeply distressed and in great personal need, physically,
spiritually, and psychologically. In the middle of the psalm he offers
his own interpretation: 'You have taken me up and thrown me aside.'
He felt that God had rejected and deserted him. He was neither the
first nor the last to do so.

But if we are going to read this psalm aright we must ask: Was this
the true interpretation of his situation? Does God forsake his faithful
people?[3] The answer must, surely, be 'No'. Not according to Psalm
118:6 and Hebrews 13:5: 'I will never leave you nor forsake you.' The
psalmist's mind has been unhinged from the truth. His perception
of God has been distorted. His basic need, therefore, is to have his
understanding of the character of God biblically recalibrated. And this
is exactly what begins to happen—again without explanation—in the
second half of the psalm:

> But you, O LORD, are enthroned forever;
> You are remembered throughout all generations.
> You will arise and have pity …[4]

He has had a distorted picture of God. The spiritual therapy he
needs, and receives, comes only when biblical truth illumines his
understanding. God is a covenant-keeping God. He never treats
his children like discarded Christmas presents. Now the psalmist
begins to apply the truth about God to his own situation. The psalm

[1] *Job* 1: 1, 8; 2:1-7.
[2] *Psa.* 102:14, 16.
[3] *Psa.* 102 is traditionally placed among the 'penitential psalms' (*Psa.* 6; 32; 38; 51;
102; 130; 143 listed as early as the sixth century by the statesman and scholar Cassi-
odorus). But this almost certainly is a category mistake since there is no confession
of sin or discovery of forgiveness in this psalm. The psalmist is of course a sinner, but
it is not his own sin or its forgiveness that is the focus of concern here.
[4] *Psa.* 102:12-13.

ends—not without further struggles on the way—with a man who had despaired of life now looking forward to God's blessing on his grandchildren![1]

When we study such a passage with any empathy for its powerful poetic language, we find ourselves drawn in to the psalmist's experience. This is the dark night of his soul. He pours out all the noxious poisons of his mis-description of God's character and ways. Now he has nothing left but the God who is; he grasps who he really is, and rests in his sovereignty and in his loyal love.

In fact the psalmist has been caught up in the conflicts and tensions promised in Genesis 3:15. What Paul evocatively calls 'the lie about God' had poisoned his mind. Now biblical truth breaks in. His vision clears, life is reinterpreted in the light of the truth. Peace returns, hope sings.

As a result of being caught up to share in what the psalmist writes we find that God's word cleanses our thinking, refreshes our emotions, and also equips us to help and encourage others whose present experience tallies with the first half rather than the second half of the psalm.

Psalm 89 provides another, perhaps simpler, example. It is the psalm of the covenant with David.[2] But the complaint of the writer is: 'You have renounced the covenant with your servant and have defiled his crown in the dust'.[3]

But had God been unfaithful to his covenant? Is God ever unfaithful to his covenant? Surely not! The principle of God's absolute faithfulness must therefore guide how we interpret the psalmist's situation. Now, as New Testament Christians, we read the psalms in the light of the fulfilment of God's covenant in Christ: 'For all the promises of God find their Yes in him.'[4] Indeed, God did not fail to keep his promise to bring believers covenant blessing even though it meant seeing his own Son bear the covenant judgment.[5]

We must read the Bible with our eyes open. The fact that its ultimate author is infallible does not mean that everything said by participants in its drama is similarly infallible. We would not read any

[1] *Psa.* 102: 28.
[2] *Psa.* 89:3, 28, 34 *etc.*
[3] *Psa.* 89:39.
[4] *2 Cor.* 1:20.
[5] *Gal.* 3:13; *Eph.* 1:3 ff.

other book that way. We should not fall into that trap when we read Scripture. It is, after all, a record of human failure and defeat as well as of divine success and triumph.

Much more could be said about reading the psalms. But one thing should not be omitted. Indeed it is paramount. Jesus used the psalms. So one of the most helpful questions a Christian can ask when reading them is: 'How would Jesus have read and applied this psalm?'

Jesus knew and loved the psalms. He would have learned them by heart as a child. So the answer to the question 'How did Jesus use the psalms?' is at one level 'The same way we use them—as expressions of prayer and praise to his Father and also as prayers of supplication to his Father'. He also saw that some of the psalms very specifically spoke about the Messiah. They stretched beyond anything the king of Israel experienced to the King who was to come, who would be born of the house of David and whose kingdom would reach the ends of the earth and extend until the end of time. Thus Jesus would read Psalm 2, with its promise of enthronement and world-wide reign, as well as Psalms 72 and 110, and reflect on God's purposes in and through his own life.

But—to turn to it once again—what of Psalm 102 which we have already seen describing the dark night of the psalmist's soul? Paradoxically Jesus is the one 'believer' for whom this entire psalm is true. On the cross the words of Psalm 102:10 were fulfilled:

> because of your indignation and anger;
>> for you have taken me up and thrown me down.

As our Lord Jesus took the place of sinners on the cross this was his experience. It is the reason why we need never experience it. But more than that, God heard his cry:

> Do not hide your face from me
>> in the day of my distress
> Incline your ear to me
>> answer me speedily in the day when I call.[1]

Indeed, only when we read these words through the lenses of the gospel do we fully appreciate their significance and power.

What then of the penitential psalms? The words of Psalm 51 cannot be placed in the mouth of the Saviour, can they?

---

[1] *Psa.* 102:2.

> Against you, you only have I sinned
> and done what is evil in your sight ...[1]

Here the relationship is different. David has committed sins for which there is no atoning sacrifice under the law. Yet he is asking God to have mercy[2] and to deliver him from condemnation.[3] He is so desperate he does not seem to realise what he is asking—for God to provide a new sacrifice to bear his judgment. In essence he is asking 'Let someone else take the guilt and condemnation of my sin.'

In a sense this is the deepest moment in the Old Testament. For David has discovered what in fact has always been the case: an animal is an inadequate sacrifice for a man's sins.[4] In this sense the psalm is a heart-cry for the coming of Christ. In this sense Jesus could read and apply this psalm to himself: 'I am the sacrifice David needed'.

But what of the so called 'Vengeance' or 'Imprecatory' Psalms—like Psalm 139:19-22?

> Oh that you would slay the wicked, O God!
> O men of blood, depart from me!
> They speak against you with malicious intent;
> your enemies take your name in vain.
> Do I not hate those who hate you, O LORD?
> And do I not loathe those who rise up against you?
> I hate them with complete hatred;
> I count them my enemies

Would Jesus have prayed like this? Can we pray like this?

Christians have never been able to reach complete agreement about how to read these psalms. Should we, perhaps, read them in the same way we have read Psalm 102:10—and say that in the God-breathed word we find a true (inerrant!) account of what men have said in their misunderstanding of the ways of God?

---

[1] *Psa.* 51:4.
[2] *Psa.* 51:1.
[3] *Psa.* 51:14.
[4] *Heb.* 9:11-12. While the viewpoint here is that of a New Testament author a believing Israelite would have been able to use the same argument as he realised that (a) animals are not adequate sacrifices for human sins, and (b) the repetition of these sacrifices indicates that they cannot be the sacrifice that will remove condemnation once and for all.

Perhaps. But some basic principles can help us towards a better understanding of how these psalms function in Scripture.

First, we need to set them within the covenant context of the whole of the Old Testament. Embedded in the birth of the people of God was God's covenant promise to Abram:

> I will make of you a great nation, and I will bless you and make your name great, so that you will be a blessing. I will bless those who bless you, *and him who dishonours you I will curse*, and in you all the families of the earth will be blessed.[1]

If the Lord's purpose for the nations is opposed and communities are irreversibly committed to destroy his people, then it may well be that only the destruction of his enemies will preserve God's blessing for the world. In this sense the psalmist's prayer is rooted in his longing for God's covenant promise to be fulfilled.[2]

Would it have been wrong in the early 1940s, for example, to pray of Hitler and his designs of 'ethnic cleansing', 'Oh that you would slay the wicked, O God!'? There were few people among the Allied Nations who thought otherwise.

Second, we need to relate some of these imprecatory prayers to the judgments that God announces through the prophets. Take the words of Psalm 137, for example—

> Remember, O Lord, against the Edomites
>   the day of Jerusalem
> how they said, 'Lay it bare, lay it bare,
>   down to its foundations!'
> O daughter of Babylon, doomed to be destroyed,
>   blessed shall he be who repays you
>   with what you have done to us!
> Blessed shall he be who takes your little ones
>   and dashes them against the rock![3]

These fearful words need to be read within the context of the prophetic judgment on Edom and Babylon in Isaiah 13:16 and against the background of the covenant promise of blessing to the nations.

---

[1] *Gen.* 12:1-3, emphasis added.
[2] In this sense, Psalm 2 stands behind the entire Book of Psalms.
[3] *Psa.* 137:7-9.

The psalmist here is simply applying the divine judgment to a situation in which the greatest of God's promises is on the verge of utter destruction.

Third, we need to distinguish between how we react to and pray for those who oppose and persecute us as individuals and the imprecatory psalms. The Scriptures teach us never to seek personal revenge.[1]

Fourth, we need to remember that while Jesus prayed for those who crucified him ('Father, forgive them') it was because they did it in ignorance.[2] He himself was being made sin for us and in that sense coming under the imprecation of God.[3] Yet this same Jesus will come again in heart-stopping and mouth-closing judgment on sinful humanity. The divine imprecation will be fulfilled by his actions:

> When the Son of Man comes in his glory … he will sit on his glorious throne. Before him will be gathered all the nations … he will place the sheep on his right, but the goats on his left …
>
> Then he will say to those on his left, 'Depart from me, you cursed, into the eternal fire prepared for the devil and his angels. For I was hungry and you gave me no food, I was thirsty and you gave me no drink …' Then they also will answer, saying, 'Lord, when did we see you hungry or thirsty … and did not minister to you?' Then he will answer them, saying, 'Truly, I say to you, as you did not do it to one of the least of these, you did not do it to me.' And these will go away into eternal punishment …[4]

Later, in the Apocalypse of John, the man we call 'the apostle of love' describes a day when all overtures of forgiveness through faith in Christ will fall silent. Then those who have stubbornly refused the way of salvation God has provided in Christ, and resisted his blessing of the nations, will experience an apocalypse of their folly.[5] On that day the meaning of the imprecatory psalms will become clear. They are

---

[1] *Matt.* 5:38-42; *Rom.* 12:7-21.

[2] *Luke* 23:34; cf. *1 Cor.* 2:8.

[3] *2 Cor.* 5:21; *Gal.* 3:13.

[4] *Matt.* 25:31-46.

[5] Notice the parallel here to *Rom.* 1:16-18: the saving power of God is revealed in the gospel; but the same God's wrath is revealed against those who stubbornly refuse and reject it.

appeals to God to preserve his salvation-expressing and grace-offering kingdom in this world by bringing forward a measure of his last-day judgments into the present day, for the sake of his own glory. The redeemed and holy martyrs in heaven pray in this way:

> O Sovereign Lord, Holy and True, how long before you will judge and avenge our blood on those who dwell on the earth?[1]

On that day (for which the redeemed must wait a little longer[2]), John tells us, it will come to pass that,

> The kings of the earth and the great ones and the generals and the rich and the powerful and everyone, slave and free, hid themselves in the caves and among the rocks of the mountains, calling to the mountains and rocks, 'Fall on us, and hide us from the face of him who is seated on the throne, and from the wrath of the Lamb, for the great day of their wrath has come, and who can stand?'[3]

There is such a reality as 'the wrath of the Lamb' and a Day when the prayer of the saints 'Your kingdom come, your will be done on earth as it is in heaven' will be fully and finally answered. Until that Day the Christian's instinct will surely be to pray 'Forgive us our sins, for we ourselves forgive everyone who is indebted to us.'[4]

As believers, then, we do not rashly (or worse, alas, arrogantly) pray down imprecations on people who oppose us and defend our bitter spirit by saying 'I am simply doing what the Bible says believers do.' We are not justified in calling people 'hypocrites' or 'whitewashed sepulchres' or using edgy language simply because Scripture occasionally does. For Scripture does this *rarely and in very specific circumstances*. Carelessness here ignores and transgresses the apostolic principle of 'rightly handling the word of truth'. We should indeed be 'ashamed' if we do that.[5] A misinterpreted and misapplied text is not the word of God.

---

[1] *Rev.* 6:10.
[2] *Rev.* 6:11.
[3] *Rev.* 6:12-17.
[4] *Luke* 11:4.
[5] *2 Tim.* 2:15.

So, when persecuted as individuals our calling is to follow Jesus' example and to share Stephen's request, 'Lord, do not hold this sin against them.'[1] Our privilege is to pray that the Lord may yet bless any Sauls of Tarsus who persecute us because 'although a blasphemer, persecutor, and insolent opponent' they may yet receive mercy because like their predecessor they 'acted ignorantly in unbelief'.[2]

We can safely leave final judgment to the Lord. For Scripture affirms that it will come on all who stubbornly and irrevocably sin against the Holy Spirit and seek to destroy the gracious promises of God. If we find ourselves in contexts where evil forces are annihilating God's church, then it may be the time to ask him to bring forward a measure of his final judgment in order to deliver the oppressed and save the nations. The integrity of our desire for his glory and the blessing of the nations will then be tested by our response if, instead, God chooses to show mercy. Then will we—unlike Jonah—be the first to praise him?

Wisdom

Various sections of the Old Testament contain what is usually called 'wisdom literature'.

God is wise. He knows the best way to achieve the best outcomes. He displayed his wisdom in creation, in the multifaceted cosmos he brought into being. He displays wisdom in his providence, in the complex ways in which he weaves together the strands of history and our personal lives to bring about his purpose. He showed his wisdom in the death and resurrection of Christ, demonstrating his love while expressing his absolute justice.[3] He shows his wisdom in the church in the way he brings together male and female, young and old, rich and poor, wise and simple, Jew and Gentile in a community that displays his multicoloured glory.[4]

But what is 'wisdom literature'? It is literature that teaches us how to live as God's covenant children in a world that has alienated itself from both his love and his laws.

---

[1] *Acts* 7:60.
[2] *1 Tim.* 1:13.
[3] *Rom.* 3:21-26; 5:6-9.
[4] *Eph.* 3:8-10.

Proverbs

Proverbs exemplifies this genre. It teaches us that the fear of the Lord, reverent faith in the covenant making and covenant keeping Lord, is where wisdom begins.[1] The first third of the book is devoted to a series of extended lessons which are then followed by a collection of pithy descriptions of how wisdom works, why we need it, and the repercussions of despising it.

The opening nine chapters of Proverbs suggest it was a book compiled to help younger people find their way in a fallen world—and perhaps to help their parents guide them. The central theme is: How to be a faithful child of God, living in the light of his covenant, in a rebellious and fallen world.

These early chapters read like a series of heart-to-heart talks, in which a wise father is helping his son[2] to see that enjoying the blessings of God's covenant promises depends on living within his covenant directives. Ignore or reject the Maker's instructions and the life we construct will be a distortion of his intentions for our peace and joy, and will ultimately lead to disaster in this world or the next.

Talks on sexual purity

A major element in these 'talks' is sexual purity.

The ancients had a proverb: *Corruptio optimi pessimum est* (the worst is the corruption of the best). So here. The Bible is not 'anti-sex'. In fact it sees the love between a man and a woman, and the intimacy possible within marriage, as one of God's crowning gifts.

In Genesis 2 all that was lacking to perfect the goodness of God's gifts to Adam was ... a woman to be his wife, companion, and friend. It should not surprise us, therefore, that the purity and happiness of this relationship—and of the family life that flowed from it—became the first object of Satan's attack. How tragic that two people who have pledged undying love for one another later find their relationship so corrupted that they cannot tolerate being in the same room together!

Both Scripture and history provide evidence that love between a man and a woman, marriage, and the family life that flows from it, are

[1] *Prov.* 1:1-7.

[2] It is not difficult to see how their principles could be worked out in a mother-daughter conversation.

central targets for satanic opposition. A distorted use of sexual desire is a major weapon in his artillery. So we need to be wise enough to say a resounding 'No' to anyone and anything that might divert us from the Maker's instructions. Hollywood's image of serial sexual relationships may appear to be attractive, but this is achieved by air-brushing. The serialism is itself an indication of lost satisfaction.

Proverbs offers wisdom for life on a much wider front than this of course. It therefore does two things. It shows us in practical detail how faithfulness to God's covenant can be worked out into daily life. And in addition it shows us some of the ways Satan seeks to divert us from God and destroy us.

The bulk of the book therefore contains a series of observations on how life works in a fallen world and how to negotiate it as a believer who knows that he is still a sinner. It is not a book of guarantees, blank cheques promising prosperity, riches, and a carefree life to anyone who puts the right coins into the slot machine. Rather it provides wise and workable principles that need to be pursued in faith as we express God's lordship in the whole of life.

Prophecy

The books of the Prophets contain sections of historical narrative. But they are much more than narrative. The prophet was a man who had stood in the presence of God and to whom God disclosed his 'secrets'.[1] The unveiling of these 'secrets' might lead to the prophet 'fore-telling' the future (revealing things that had not yet taken place). But more typically it involved 'forth-telling'—applying the word that God had already spoken to contemporary or coming circumstances and times.

In this connection recall that the historical books Joshua, Judges, Samuel, and Kings were also classified as prophetic. They interpreted all events from the perspective of Scripture or *Torah* and saw the specific history of God's people working out in terms of the principles of that covenant recorded in Deuteronomy 27-30.

Here, then, is an important principle to understand: *narratives in Scripture are never neutral*. They read and interpret 'history' from the standpoint of God's covenant, with its promises of blessings to the obedience of faith and judgment curses on unbelief and disobedience.

[1] *Amos* 3:7.

God always remains faithful to his word—but the implications of that faithfulness are integrated with the response of his people.

'Prophecy' therefore is, ultimately, the declaration, exposition, and application of God's covenant word.

It may take the form of an analysis of *the past* ('prophetic history').

It may involve the application of God's covenant word to *the present*, for example in the lawsuit style (Hebrew *rîb*) of denunciations common in the Prophets; or

It may expound how God's covenant word will be fulfilled in new ways *in the future*. Usually the prophet will express what is yet to take place in terms of realities he and the people already experience and understand. This is why prophecy's fulfilment lies in events which, in various ways, transcend the framework of the language in which they were originally given.

As Christians of course we are now able to read the prophets in the light of the fulfilment of God's promises in Christ:

> Long ago, at many times and in many ways, God spoke to our fathers by the prophets, but in these last days he has spoken to us by his Son …[1]

When we read prophecy, we must bear in mind three things.

First, prophecy was given in a particular context in the past. To be understood it must be seen against that background. The first question to ask is: What did this passage say, and what was it meant to do, in the situation in which it was first spoken or read?

Second, prophecy is often conditional.[2] On occasion it is a summons back to God's word which, if ignored, will unleash the promised judgment of God. But if God's word effects repentance, and is obeyed, the windows of heaven will be opened and blessing for God's people restored.[3]

Third, the prophets inevitably clothed their teaching in the thought forms and ideas of their own time. Otherwise what they said would have been totally unintelligible. Their description of what God would

---

[1] *Heb.* 1:1-2.
[2] See, *e.g.*, *1 Kings* 21:17 ff; *Jer.* 26:17 ff; *Ezek.* 18:1-24; *Jon.* 3:4 ff.
[3] *Mal.* 3:10-12.

bring about in the future was inevitably expressed in terms of the cultural and religious traditions under which they lived. The fulfilment connects to the prophecy, but is also a *fill-full-ment*.

We see this illustrated in the way in which the apostles saw the fulfilment of certain Old Testament prophecies.[1] For that reason it is both legitimate and necessary to understand their statements in terms of the ways in which the New Testament itself sees them fulfilled.

The New Testament's account of how the apostles interpreted and applied Amos 9:11-12 illustrates this:

> 'In that day I will raise up
> the booth of David that is fallen
> and repair its breaches,
> and raise up its ruins
> and rebuild it as in the days of old,
> that they may possess the remnant of Edom
> and all the nations who are called by my name,'
> declares the LORD who does this.

At first sight these words have a plain meaning. They seem to refer to the national, indeed physical, restoration of Jerusalem, and to a programme of national expansion and prosperity.

Many Christians believe that God still has some future purpose for the Jewish people, and for the land of Israel. Some (but by no means all of them) therefore understand these words to refer to that future period.

When the apostles and elders met in Jerusalem to hear Peter's plea for, and Paul and Barnabas's account of, the evangelization of the Gentiles, this passage was quoted as a major factor in the final decision.[2] James stated that the evangelization of the Gentiles was in agreement with these words. He thus understood them to refer not to some future ingathering of the Jews, but to the post-Pentecost ingathering of the Gentiles.

Clearly the apostles interpreted and applied the words of Amos as a prophecy of events in the new age described in terms of the world of the old age.

[1] Presumably they learned to do this from remembering Jesus' teaching during his ministry and with the benefit of the 'Bible study' he did with them from Easter Sunday until Ascension Day. See *Luke* 24:27, 44-49; *Acts* 1:1-3.

[2] *Acts* 15:1-35. The Amos prophecy is cited in 15:16-17.

This is not to say that God has no further purpose for the Jewish people.[1] It is only to say that this is not the truth taught by this particular passage. James applied Amos's words to the church, and the visible prosperity of the spiritual kingdom of God, not to the literal, ethnic nation of Israel. Since in the days of Amos the nation and the church were, theoretically, two sides of the same coin, the prophet inevitably expressed himself in language which reflected the 'old' order. James transposed it into the new covenant key.

Paying attention to how the apostles applied prophecy—something which they must have learned from the Lord Jesus himself—is therefore the key to our ability to do the same.

---

[1] Many students of Scripture have concluded that *Rom.* 11:1-32 teach that God has such an ongoing purpose for the Jewish people.

7. Gospels, Epistles, and Visions

A page with only three words printed on it separates the Hebrew Scriptures from 'The New Testament'. That page represents the passage of some four hundred years. Most of what follows records the events of not much more than a generation. Whereas the Old Testament took centuries to write, the twenty-seven books that follow it were completed within a single life span.

Yet these differences in themselves do not explain why the gap in atmosphere between the Old and the New feels so great. After all there are four centuries between David and Daniel. We feel we are in the same world when we read about these two heroes of the faith.

But when we turn the blank page and read 'The book of the genealogy of Jesus Christ, the son of David, the son of Abraham', we know we have taken a step into a new world order altogether. Nobody in the Old Testament is described as Jesus is. *Events of epoch-making proportions have clearly taken place.*

Later we learn that now (*i.e.* since the incarnation, life, death, resurrection, and ascension of Jesus) gender barriers have been broken down, ethnic differences have been flattened; God's people no longer need prophets, priests, or kings; believers call God 'Abba, Father'; resurrection and new life form the melody line of everything that follows.

The difference in atmosphere, teaching, hope, personal focus, and even in the kind of literature is so dramatic that only familiarity causes us to miss it.

We are lacking in sensitivity, therefore, if we are surprised that the coming of the gospel brought in its wake the writing of the New Testament. The old covenant came with its own covenant documents, telling the story of its formation and outworking through the many centuries of Old Testament history. The new covenant, with its fuller, greater, consummating revelation comes with similar documents. They tell the story of the forging of the new covenant in Christ (Gospels), its early progress (Acts of the Apostles), its application in the lives of the first churches (Epistles), and its certain future triumph (Revelation).

In the New Testament we therefore find literature that parallels that of the Old.

There is narrative history. It is told now not from a perspective centred on God's covenant promise, but on the person of Christ who embodies God's covenant in himself.

There is also material that parallels the Prophets, now written in the form of epistles or letters. These letters are, for all practical purposes, written preaching.[1]

There is visionary, or apocalyptic material, lifting the veil that separates earth from heaven and the present from the future, found largely in the book of Revelation.

In this chapter we will consider some of the clues we need if we are going to read these varying types of literature properly and profitably.

Gospels

The Gospels are narrative histories of a particular kind. They are not biographies but Gospels. They do not simply record facts; they are written proclamations that Jesus of Nazareth is Saviour and Lord.

Each Gospel is shaped by the author who wrote it and the context in which and for which it was written. They do not contradict each other, but each author tells the story in a slightly different way, selecting[2] and arranging the material in a way that best fits his purpose and intended audience.

Christians tend to be more familiar with the Gospels than with, for example, Hebrews or Galatians. We also tend to think they are much easier to understand because they are narratives. But, perhaps

---

[1] Paul saw his preaching and his letters as two aspects of the same authoritative apostolic ministry, 'forth-telling' and 'fore-telling', the word of God. See 2 *Thess.* 2:15.

[2] 'Selecting' since John tells us, with presumably a smile playing on his lips, that 'Were every one of them [*i.e.* the things that Jesus did] to be written, I suppose that the world itself could not contain the books that would be written' (*John* 21:25).

surprisingly, when we read them we often forget a basic principle: *When you read the Gospels, don't lose sight of Jesus; keep your eyes fixed on him.*

Is it even necessary to say this? Yes, indeed!

Sometimes Christians seem to be looking primarily for themselves when reading the Gospels, in the sense that their first questions tend to be: 'Who am I like in this story? What does it say *to me?*' This is often nurtured in group Bible studies by leaders whose first question is 'Now, what is this passage saying *to you?*' Thus, for example, in reading the story of Jesus' encounter with Zacchaeus we ask, 'How am I like Zacchaeus?' (Or Bartimaeus, or Mary or Martha, or Peter, or …).

But the Gospels are not, in the first instance, 'about' Zacchaeus, Bartimaeus, Mary, Martha or Peter! And they are certainly not about 'me'! They are about Jesus Christ. So our first question therefore should never be: 'What does this passage tell me about me?' but 'What does this passage tell me about the Lord Jesus?' Then, knowing that he is 'the same yesterday, today and forever'[1] enables us to say: He remains the same for us today. What Jesus is in any of the Gospel narratives, he always is. But only when we have first fixed our focus on what Jesus was 'yesterday' (during his ministry), will we discover what he is 'today' (since his resurrection, ascension and the day of Pentecost), and therefore 'forever' (not only today, but tomorrow, and indeed for all eternity).

Like the 'Ephesians Test' mentioned in chapter 4, we need to be familiar with the 'Gospels Test'. When we have finished reading through any of the Gospels we should, at the very least, be able to tell someone

- What Jesus did;
- What Jesus taught;
- Who Jesus is; and
- What it means to be his disciple.

If, after years of reading the Gospels, all I know is a few isolated and disconnected texts that have helped me through the day, I may have missed the point of the Gospels by exchanging long-term benefits for short-term gains. Of course the Gospels instruct, guide, encourage,

[1] *Heb.* 13:8.

and help us day by day. But becoming familiar with what they say in these different ways about the Lord Jesus will be a much more significant help to us than treating them as a promise-box of isolated verses.

Matthew provides us with an important key to understanding the ministry of Jesus:

Jesus had recently been baptized, affirmed as the Son of God, and anointed for his royal ministry as the Suffering Servant Messiah.[1]

He had then been led by the Spirit to confront and defeat the devil in the wilderness.[2]

He had then moved to live in Capernaum and begun to preach his message of the kingdom of heaven.[3]

He had begun to call his disciples.[4]

> And he went throughout all Galilee, teaching in their synagogues and proclaiming the gospel of the kingdom and healing every disease and every affliction among the people.[5]

Here are the main features of Jesus' ministry. Anointed as the Royal King, Priest, and Prophet, he had engaged the devil in moral conflict and defeated him, thus reversing what had taken place in the Garden of Eden. He then announced that the kingdom of God (or heaven) had arrived, because he—the King—had come. He had established a bridgehead into the devil's territory and was about to make more inroads by calling Simon and Andrew, James and John.

He then established the pattern of his ministry:

- He taught, proclaiming the gospel of the kingdom. Matthew gives us an immediate illustration in the three chapters that follow in the Sermon on the Mount.[6] Whenever he taught he would weave parables into his preaching.[7]

- He healed the sick, and thus indicated that he had come to reverse the effects of the fall.

---

[1] *Matt.* 3:13-17.
[2] *Matt.* 4:1-11.
[3] *Matt.* 4:12-17.
[4] *Matt.* 4:18-22.
[5] *Matt.* 4:23.
[6] *Matt.* chapters 5, 6, 7.
[7] *Matt.* 13:34.

• He delivered those who were oppressed by demons,[1] demonstrating that he had won a signal victory over their master the devil.

His teaching, then, was characterised by parables and miracles. And so, woven into the narrative of the first three Gospels[2] we find an entire series of both. If we are to appreciate the Gospels we need to understand how they function as expressions of Christ's kingdom.

Parables

The interpretation of parables has been a happy hunting ground for misunderstandings. One common misunderstanding is assuming that by telling parables Jesus was using illustrations for his sermons. Certainly the parables illustrate. But there is more to them than that. The reason for using a sermon illustration is to make the message clearer. But Jesus himself underscored that the function of his parables is to test whether or not the message *is* clear to the hearer. For parables can either illumine or blind us.[3]

Allegories?

Throughout the history of the church there has been a temptation to focus on the details of a parable to such an extent that the context in which it is told and the punch line with which it ends are ignored. The 'allegorical' approach to reading Scripture often surfaced here, and to varying degrees continues to be used.

An allegory is a narrative in which the main details of a story represent realities in the world in which we live. John Bunyan's great book *The Pilgrim's Progress* is by far the best-known Christian example. People and places in an obviously fictional world represent character types and categories of experience in the 'real world'.[4]

---

[1] *Matt.* 4:24.

[2] The first three Gospels are often referred to as the 'Synoptic' Gospels because they share a common perspective, and indeed seem to be dependent on a common body of information. John's Gospel, which unlike the first three begins the story in eternity, is written from a different perspective.

[3] As he makes clear in *Matt.* 13:13-15.

[4] It should be said here that the most influential interpreters in the modern era have tended to stress that parables are not allegories and that in essence each parable

We have already seen that allegorical or 'spiritual' interpretation goes back to the Hellenistic world into which the gospel was first preached.[1] Perhaps it is not too surprising that some who were converted from that environment read the Bible in this way too. The 'literal' sense of a passage stood on lower ground than the 'spiritual'. In keeping with this an allegorical reading of any text was always 'higher' than a literal one. In a sense the misstep being made was to look for *application* (What is the gospel? What doctrines appear here in code form? How does this explain the Christian life?) without a proper context-sensitive *interpretation*. The *application* was then treated as though it were the *interpretation*.

Among the earliest Christian writers Origen of Alexandria (A.D. 185-254) is best known for employing this approach to the Bible as a whole, and to parables in particular.

Here is the parable of the good Samaritan:

> And behold, a lawyer stood up to put him to the test, saying, 'Teacher, what shall I do to inherit eternal life?' He said to him, 'What is written in the Law? How do you read it?' And he answered, 'You shall love the Lord your God with all your heart and with all your soul and with all your strength and with all your mind, and your neighbour as yourself.' And he said to him, 'You have answered correctly; do this, and you will live.'
>
> But he, desiring to justify himself, said to Jesus, 'And who is my neighbour?' Jesus replied, 'A man was going down from Jerusalem to Jericho, and he fell among robbers, who stripped him and beat him and departed, leaving him half dead. Now by chance a priest was going down that road, and when he saw him he passed by on the other side. So likewise

---

makes only one major point. More recently a number of fine scholars have contested this and argued that in fact the parables *are* allegories. This view should not be confused with the allegorical method of interpretation. It is arguing that we should recognise that the parables are allegories and therefore we should interpret them as allegories. Of course much depends on how we answer the question 'What, exactly, *is* an allegory?' My own view is that the difference between a parable and what is usually described as an allegory is that the former tells a story from the real world in which the unexpected takes place, whereas the latter tells a story from what is *obviously* a fictional world to illustrate life in the real world.

[1] See above, p. 66.

a Levite, when he came to the place and saw him, passed by on the other side. But a Samaritan, as he journeyed, came to where he was, and when he saw him, he had compassion. He went to him and bound up his wounds, pouring on oil and wine. Then he set him on his own animal and brought him to an inn and took care of him. And the next day he took out two denarii and gave them to the innkeeper, saying, "Take care of him, and whatever more you spend, I will repay you when I come back." Which of these three, do you think, proved to be a neighbour to the man who fell among the robbers?' He said, 'The one who showed him mercy.' And Jesus said to him, 'You go, and do likewise.'[1]

Here is Origen's interpretation:

Jerusalem represents heaven.

The man travelling from Jerusalem to Jericho is Adam.

Jericho represents the world.

The thieves who set upon the man are the devil and his emissaries.

The priest who passes by is the Law which is powerless to help.

The Levite stands for the Prophets who cannot save the man.

The Good Samaritan is … Christ himself.

The beast on which he places the man is the body of Christ in which he bears our sins.

The inn where the man is lodged is the church.

The innkeeper represents the angel who is in charge of the church.

The two coins given to the innkeeper represent the knowledge of the Father and the Son.

The Samaritan's promise to return represents the second coming of Christ.[2]

This general approach became relatively commonplace. But notice how it loses focus on Jesus' 'punch-line' 'You go and do likewise.'

[1] *Luke* 10:25-37.

[2] See Origen, *Homilies on Luke*, tr. and ed. Joseph T. Lienhard (Washington, DC: Catholic University of America Press, 1996), pp. 137-141.

But by what principles can we judge between this interpretation and other suggestions made using the same method? Augustine's view was that the innkeeper is the apostle Paul and that the two pennies represent the two great commands to love. Which is correct? Nothing in the text itself helps us to decide. There seem to be too few controls built into this approach.

These interpretations are ingenious, yes. And they have their attractions. But they presuppose that the parable is meant to be an abbreviated systematic theology. It is almost like a quiz show with Jesus as the host and ourselves as contestants. We are shown various pictures. Behind each picture lies a doctrine. The 'game' is called 'Guess the Doctrine'.

But Jesus did not say, at the close of the parable, 'Now, did you get the right doctrine?' No, he was testing the lawyer's heart. He was subverting his assumptions. He was exposing him because he knew he was 'desiring to justify himself'. The parable is not a picture puzzle representing all the doctrines of the gospel. It is a story about how the inbreaking of the kingdom turns the world of self-justifying people upside down.

How is this? In a brilliant *tour de force* Jesus turned the question ('Who *is* my neighbour?') back on the questioner, by asking 'Who *showed himself to be a neighbour?*' Then, receiving the right answer ('The one who showed him mercy'), Jesus pressed home the application to the self-justifying lawyer: 'You go, and do likewise!' A man who wanted to limit his responsibilities ('Tell me who I should love and let me draw my own conclusions about those I do not need to love') had the ground taken from underneath his feet. Wherever there is need *that* is the place where you are to become a neighbour! *That*, not finding how to limit our responsibilities, is kingdom life.

So parables are not intended to be read as though they were allegories in which each feature of the story has a one-to-one parallel in Christian theology or experience. Most of the details are intended to 'set the scene', to convey the general atmosphere in which the message of the parable will strike home to both the understanding and the emotions of its hearer. If we confuse the issues by puzzling over doctrinal equivalents we may find ourselves among those who 'seeing do not see, and hearing do not hear'.[1]

[1] *Matt.* 13:13.

Parable principles

We can take it as a general rule of thumb that parables paint pictures of something unexpected in life which—often with marvellous attention to literary details that enhance the emotional power of the narrative—teach us how God's kingdom works. They bring us into a kingdom where Samaritans help Jews, where prodigal sons are welcomed home, and much else happens to overturn our expectations.

With this in mind, there are two things for which we should look as we read them.

The scope of the parable. What, in general terms, is it saying? The occasion on which the parable was told normally helps us here.

The parable of the good Samaritan illustrates this well. It was not merely a moral tale about helping your neighbour. We are deliberately told the heart-motivation of the lawyer who asked the question. We should therefore anticipate that the parable would expose his heart, and rip away his self-justification. He laid bare his defence mechanisms. His question had been 'Who is my neighbour?' Jesus' reply, essentially, was: 'You are asking the wrong question. You are a man with a bad heart. The kingdom of God has arrived. I have come as its King, reversing all the false values and lifestyles of this world. Believe the good news and live the repentant life in which those values are turned upside down so that you are willing to meet needs wherever they are found'.[1]

Sometimes a parable's purpose is made explicit in the introduction. Thus: 'And he told them a parable to the effect that *they ought always to pray and not lose heart'.*[2] Here we only need to read what is said to know what the general point of the parable is going to be.

Alternatively, it may be expressed in its closing words.[3] Thus Jesus

---

[1] By way of personal testimony to the challenge of Jesus' words, a number of years ago at a lunch hour gathering in our church I ended a message on this parable by saying that having heard these words of Jesus I felt sure some of us would be tested on them within the coming week. Later that day as I walked across the churchyard to the mid-week prayer meeting I saw through the gloom what looked like a large object lying on the ground. It was a homeless man, lying asleep on a cold night. I should have known that I would be the first one to be tested!

[2] *Luke* 18:1.

[3] This is sometimes referred to as 'the principle of end stress'. It is not unique to Jesus' parables of course. As many a joke-teller knows to his or her cost, confuse the

concludes his story of the friend at midnight: 'And I tell you, ask, and it will be given to you; seek, and you will find; knock, and it will be opened to you.'[1] Similarly the message of the rich fool is applied in these solemn terms: 'So is the one who lays up treasure for himself and is not rich toward God.'[2]

Notice these hints and we are well on our way to understanding the point which is being made in a parable and applying it to our own lives.

The point of comparison. Many parables are explicitly described as 'parables of the kingdom'. They begin with the words, 'The kingdom of God [or heaven] is *like* …' We should therefore ask: 'What exactly is the point of comparison here?' It may be the manner in which the kingdom is established. It may be an illustration of the principles which are involved in the life of the kingdom, such as consecration, prayerfulness, patience, boldness, wisdom, or some other quality. It may be the issue of personal decision about entry into the kingdom of God which is the thrust of the story.

Very often, the essence of the parable is: the kingdom of God operates in *this* way (illustrated in the parable); now what is your response going to be? Is it going to be like the man in the parable? Is it going to be like the first man in the parable, or the second man? (or the pathway, the rocky soil, the weed-infested soil, or the good soil?).

The parable we usually call *the prodigal son* illustrates this last point well.

Prodigal sons?

A major key to understanding the parable of the prodigal son lies in the context in which it was told and in its conclusion. It ends with the *elder* brother. This is significant. The story about the remarkable father who forgives, welcomes and restores is double-edged.

Luke chapter 15 as a whole is a triptych—a picture painted on three panels. Our Lord tells three related short stories about a lost sheep (one out of one hundred), a lost coin (one out of ten) and a lost son (ultimately one out of two). The context that gives rise to the parable

---

'punch-line' and the story falls flat!

[1] *Luke* 11:9.
[2] *Luke* 12:21.

is the complaining of the Pharisees that Jesus welcomed sinners.[1] The father's gracious restoration of the younger brother followed by the refusal of the elder brother to share in the celebration makes the hearers (and readers) ask: 'Who am I? Am I like the prodigal, a pardoned sinner? Or am I really like the elder brother, whose heart is cold towards the prodigal, because cold towards the love of the Father?

The elder brother's complaint is: 'Look! All these years I've been slaving for you and never disobeyed your orders. Yet you never gave me ... But when this son of yours who has squandered your property with prostitutes comes home, you kill the fattened calf for him!'[2] This is a deliberate echo of the muttered accusations of the Pharisees and the teachers of the law which form the context for the parable: 'This man receives sinners and eats with them.'[3]

The prodigal brother receives his father's gracious pardon, acceptance, and welcome. The elder brother is left in self-justification and estrangement. At the end of the day it is the elder brother who proves to be the prodigal. He wastes the invitation to rejoice in the father's grace and refuses what the father offered to both his sons.

There is no need to find the cross, the resurrection, justification, adoption, sanctification, or glorification here. That is not the point. The robe is a robe, the ring is a ring, the sandals are sandals, and the fattened calf that is slain is a celebratory steak dinner.

There are of course subtle layers to this story that require some understanding of the culture of the ancient near east: the 'far country' is the place of exile from God's promises; pigs are unclean animals; businessmen in the ancient near east did not run; returned prodigals were exposed to a shaming ritual, not welcomed with open arms; family members, not slaves, wore sandals in the home; rings are signs of responsibility and authority. All of the details have their own significance within the story, enhancing the marvel of the father's love. They exist to heighten our sense of wonder at Christ's grace, not to be a class quiz in 'Systematic Theology 101'.

The big story lies on the surface of the text: Christ welcomes sinners, whether lost in a pig-sty in the far country or lost in the comfort

[1] *Luke* 15:1.
[2] *Luke* 15:29-30 NIV.
[3] *Luke* 15:2.

of the father's farm. Sadly often those nearest 'home' can be furthest away from the Father. The parable is simultaneously a message of marvellous grace and compassionate warning.

In this way the parables not only describe how God's kingdom operates, and the principles of grace which pervade it; they call for a response to the King. The one thing all of the parables have in common is *the person who is telling them*. In his coming the kingdom of God has been established. At the end of the day all of the parables are about our response to him. The very process of reading or hearing them reveals what that response is.

A colleague with expertise in personal counselling once told me that he often used this diagnostic question: 'Is there a parable that irritates you?' It is an interesting technique designed to disclose whether I have a heart-problem with how Christ's kingdom operates in both grace and judgment.

The Gospels are also the part of Scripture in which miracles most frequently feature.

Miracles

What is the significance of a miracle? Once again our first task is to read each miracle in its proper biblical and theological context.

There is a tendency to use the word 'miracle' to denote any remarkable event or experience. People who do not believe in the miracles recorded in Scripture will nevertheless describe something by saying 'It was a miracle'.

The Bible itself is more discriminating in its use of the term. In its pages, not everything that is remarkable, nor even everything that is supernatural, is labelled 'miraculous'. Regeneration is a supernatural work of God; justification is a supernatural divine act. But neither is called a miracle in the New Testament.

If we review the biblical story as a whole what we discover—perhaps to our surprise—is that miracles:

> take place *infrequently*, and

> have very *specific functions* in the Bible narrative.

Contrary to a common assumption, miracles are not everyday events. They do not occur with consistent frequency in the pages of

Scripture. In fact 'miracles' performed by the servants of God tend to occur in clusters and in only a handful of periods in biblical history. Each of these clusters lasted around a generation or so:

> During the Exodus and entry into the land in the days of Moses and his lieutenant Joshua;
>
> In the days of Elijah and Elisha when the kingdom of God was threatened to the point of extinction;
>
> In the days of Daniel when that kingdom seems to have had few representatives, and
>
> In the days of Christ and the apostles.

Most of the leading figures in the Bible did not perform any 'miraculous' deed.

What is a miracle?

The New Testament uses three terms to describe miracles. They occur together in one verse (actually in one sentence) in Luke's account of the day of Pentecost:

> Jesus of Nazareth, a man attested to you by God with *mighty works* and *wonders* and *signs* that God did through him in your midst ...[1]

A miracle is:

> *dunamis*—a work of power;
>
> *teras*—a wonder;
>
> *sēmeion*—a sign.

What, then, marks out biblical miracles? Characteristically they are actions that:

> • Demonstrate the power of God in a way that causes wonder and awe;
>
> • Express his mercy to the weak and needy and his judgment on sin;
>
> • Confirm and authenticate those who inaugurate new

[1] *Acts* 2:22.

epochs of divine activity and/or are the divinely commissioned bearers of a new stage of revelation.

• Defend or advance the kingdom of God at significant epochs of its history.

• Give us brief glimpses of the way in which God will fully and finally overcome Satan and the effects of his work and restore men and women to what he intended them to be.

This is precisely what we see in the ministry of the Lord Jesus:— A miracle inaugurates his life—the virgin conception.

Thirty years later, during which he apparently performs no personal miracles, he steps onto the public stage, and is marked out as God's beloved Son and Messiah. He then immediately goes into battle against the evil one, thus inaugurating the final crisis prophesied in Genesis 3:15. Having gained his initial victory he brings the new revelation of God (as Father, Son and Holy Spirit). In his ministry he displays the grace and compassion of the kingdom by the forgiveness of sins and the restoration of lives—healing the sick, giving sight to the blind, enabling the lame to walk, the deaf to hear, and the dumb to speak.[1] He also shows the power of the kingdom by further defeats of the kingdom of darkness. He welcomes those who have been bruised and broken by the fall. And he gives glimpses of what he will fully and finally accomplish in the consummation of his kingdom. As his life began with a miracle, so after his death it begins again with another miracle—the resurrection.

Seeing Jesus' ministry in this context also explains the extent and intensity of demonic possession and oppression in the final three years of his life. Why, for example, when it takes only one demon to mete out destruction on a person's life, does Jesus encounter a man named Legion, so-called because of the vast number of demons oppressing his life? The answer is surely: because *Jesus* has come. John, although he nowhere records a case of demon possession,[2] gives the New Testament's most succinct answer: 'The reason the Son of God appeared was to destroy the works of the devil.'[3] Satan was mustering all his forces against Christ's death blow.

---

[1] See the flow of the narrative in, for example, *Luke* 4:1-44.
[2] Judas was, strictly speaking, not an exception. He was Satan-indwelt (*John* 13:2).
[3] *1 John* 3:8.

Jesus' miracles need to be interpreted in this context. He is not being held before us as an example of what Christians in the future will do, but as a once-for-all unique Conqueror. Again, the principle for interpreting and applying the Gospel account is not 'How can I do this?' but 'Who is he who does this?'[1] Here again we are drawn back to focus on the uniqueness of Christ himself.[2]

Epistles

About one third of the New Testament is made up of Letters, thirteen of them written by Paul, three by John, two by Peter, one each by James and Jude, and one other anonymously (Hebrews and I John are distinctive among the Epistles since they do not have the format of a letter as such).

What should we look out for when we read these Letters?

(1) New Testament Letters, simply because they are letters, represent one side of a two-way conversation between the apostles who wrote them and the first readers. Again we must resist the temptation to ask—as our first question—'What is this passage saying *to me?*' It was written *for me*, but not *to me*. Rather, as we explore the question 'What did this passage say to its first recipient(s)?' we will come to understand better what its message is for us.

The Epistles are long by the standard of our letters, but short by comparison with the length of other books in the Bible. It is both

---

[1] Thus the disciples were asking exactly the right question after witnessing Jesus still the storm. See *Mark* 4:41.

[2] If it is objected that Jesus said his disciples would do greater works than his (*John* 14:12), two things should be noted: (1) This is a promise to the apostles, not to Christians in general; (2) There is no record of the apostles doing greater *miracles*—for what could be greater than raising the dead? The promise of greater *works* then seems to have in view the events of Pentecost and beyond when, through the ministry of the apostles 'greater works' were done than had been witnessed in Jesus' ministry. Luke's account of events in the Jerusalem church (which began with 120 people, *Acts* 1:15) might almost give the impression he was deliberately writing his own commentary on Jesus' words: There were three thousand baptisms on the Day of Pentecost, with daily conversions following (*Acts* 2:41, 47), 'more than ever believers were added to the Lord, multitudes of both men and women' (*Acts* 5:14); 'the disciples were increasing in number ... the number of disciples multiplied greatly in Jerusalem and a great many of the priests became obedient to the faith' (*Acts* 6:1, 7); and later the church in Judea, Galilee and Samaria 'multiplied' (*Acts* 9:31). Little of this happened during Jesus' ministry.

helpful and possible to read each of them at one sitting—as they were originally intended to be read. If you do, make a simple outline of the book as you read. Further study will fill out the outline. Soon you will experience the pleasure—not to say the helpfulness—of having a working knowledge of the contents of the whole book. (Remember the Ephesians Test!). This in turn helps us to reflect on the letter's teaching even when it is not sitting open in front of us.

(2) The Letters are often described as 'occasional' writings—written in response to particular situations that arose in the young churches of the first century. So we will always come to a letter asking: 'What is the reason for writing this letter?' Often it is to rectify a problem in the life of the church, or to address areas where the author feels the gospel needs to make further progress. Making the connection between the issue addressed and the teaching that responds to it is a major clue to the way in which we apply the message to contemporary life.

(3) As we read and re-read the Letters we begin to notice that there are themes that keep reappearing. There is a pattern of response to dysfunction in the life of the church or individual. Although the problems discussed may differ from each other, there are basic starting points to the response. Paul in particular always seems to take us back to these first principles and work out his solution from them.

A first principle in Paul's Letters is the believer's union with Christ. His characteristic way of describing a 'Christian'—a rare word appearing only three times in the New Testament[1]— is to say that he or she is 'in Christ'.[2] He uses this phrase, or a variant of it, well over one hundred times. In fact his most common response to spiritual problems and malfunctions is to say—in one form or another—

> You do not seem to have grasped what it means to be a Christian. It means to be 'in Christ'—and that reality has the following implications for your life ...

What does Paul mean? In summary his thinking is as follows: By nature we are all 'in Adam'. He was not only the first man, he was also the head of the whole human race. His actions carried implications for everyone.

---

[1] *Acts* 11:26; 26:28; *1 Pet.* 4:16.

[2] The *expression* is dominantly Pauline. It occurs elsewhere in the Letters only in *1 Pet.* 3:16; 5:10, 14. But the *idea* is more pervasive.

In that sense, all of us are, by nature, 'in Adam'. And since he was the first man, the distortion of his nature in the fall has twisted human nature as a whole, bending it out of shape, releasing into it tendencies to sin.

Our situation is hopeless, and we are helpless. But God has intervened. He sent his Son to rescue us from the effects of our union with the first man, the first Adam. He became the 'Second Man', the 'Last Adam'. By his obedience he has done what the first Adam failed to do. In his death he has taken the punishment the first Adam brought upon us. So by his resurrection he has reversed the flow of death that was brought into the world by Adam's sin.[1]

The Holy Spirit works in our hearts to bring us to faith and to unite us to Christ. For Paul this is such a unique reality that it reshapes the way he uses language. On occasion he uses the preposition 'into' when he speaks about faith: we believe '*into* Christ'. The result is that we come to share in Christ's death, his resurrection, his ascension, and indeed his return in glory. This determines our identity now. We are no longer 'in Adam' living lives determined by sin and death; we are now 'in Christ' and our identity is shaped by all that he has done for us, and by the death and resurrection in which we have come to share.

Now, says Paul, we are those who, in union with Christ, have died to the reign of sin and been raised into a new realm in which Christ reigns in grace.[2] We must think about ourselves in this way.[3] As we do so we will have all the motivation we need to resist sin and to live for Christ.[4]

(4) Related to this is the way Paul expounds his message using what we might call 'Gospel Grammar'.

We have already seen how this functions. The commands and exhortations of the gospel (*imperatives*: 'You need to do that') always arise from the exposition of God's grace in the gospel (*indicatives*: 'God has done this'). Imperatives flow from indicatives, indicatives give rise to imperatives.

---

[1] Paul expounds this particularly in the key passages *Rom.* 5:12-21 and *1 Cor.* 15:20-28.

[2] *Rom.* 6:1-10. Cf. *Col.* 3:1-4.

[3] *Rom.* 6:11.

[4] *Rom.* 6:12-14. Cf. *Col.* 3:5-17.

Both Romans and Ephesians are built in their entirety on this gospel grammar structure. They can readily be divided into two sections: (i) *Indicatives*: This is what God has done in Christ for you; (ii) *Imperatives*: Since God has done all this in Christ for you, here is how you should respond with the help and in the power of the Holy Spirit.

In Romans chapters 1-11 Paul writes almost exclusively in the indicative mood:[1] Here is what God has done. Chapter 12 begins with a significant hinge word: 'therefore'—*i.e.* since all this is true, here are the implications. Chapters 12-16 then show how the gospel thus expounded works out in 'the obedience of faith'.[2] A torrent of imperatives cascades down upon the reader! But the indicatives of the gospel expounded in chapters 1-11 are able to sustain them all.

Ephesians has a similar structure. In chapters 1-3 Paul expounds the riches of God's grace towards us in Christ. At Ephesians 3:1 he is on the point of turning to application. But just as he describes himself as 'Paul, a prisoner for Christ Jesus on behalf of you Gentiles—' the astonishing nature of this self-description causes him to reflect on the gospel's wonder. He is:

A free Roman citizen willing to be bound;

A prejudiced Jew now devoted to the Gentiles;

A persecutor now turned follower of Jesus Christ.

Only then in Ephesians 4:1 does the dominant grammar of the letter change, and the indicative-imperative dynamic of gospel logic and grammar kicks into action: 'I *therefore* ... urge you'.[3]

If we turn this on its head—as though our obedience were the reason for God's grace—we would mispronounce the gospel. Always it is God's grace that grounds our obedience. The greater and richer the grace expounded the more rigorous and demanding the imperatives it is able to sustain in our lives. That is how the gospel works.

As we noted earlier, this is as true in the Old Testament as it is in the New: it is because God is the Lord who redeemed his people

---

[1] While imperatives may be implied in places, apart from a cluster of them in *Rom.* 6:12-14, they are virtually absent in *Rom.* 1-11.

[2] *Rom.* 1:5; 16:26.

[3] This is not to say that indicative statements always precede imperatives in the text. It may read *either* 'Since A is true you need to be/do B', or 'Be/do B since A is true.' In each case, however, the *logic* of the gospel remains the same.

from Egypt that they receive the imperative: 'You shall have no other gods before me.'[1]

Apocalypse

The last book of the Bible, Revelation, has a character all of its own in the New Testament. It belongs to the genre of 'Apocalyptic'.[2] In fact it is 'The Apocalypse of John'—or more accurately, on the basis of its opening words, 'An apocalypse of Jesus Christ which God gave him [i.e. John] to show to his servants …'.[3]

For many Christians the last book of the New Testament is also the most intimidating one. It abounds in strange visions, repulsive creatures, the constant use of numbers, and much else. Are there clues to help us, or handles that we can hold on to, in order to find our way through this labyrinth?

Here are some basic principles to help us read Revelation.

An *apocalypse* is not first and foremost history written in advance so that every last detail of the book stands for an event that will take place in the future. Revelation is best understood as a book of dramatic symbolic scenes. Perhaps even better it is a massive tapestry in which the details flow into the central picture and help us to make sense of it.

Revelation had a message that was relevant to its first readers. Its purpose then was not to turn them into armchair theological puzzle-solvers, but to challenge, strengthen, and encourage them in the face of persecution. This is already clear in the seven so-called 'letters to the churches' in the opening three chapters.

The book does this as a moving picture which portrays the truth of two biblical texts in dramatic form:

- The LORD God said to the serpent, …
  I will put enmity between you and the woman,
    and between your offspring and her offspring [*corporate* conflict]
  He shall bruise your head,
    and you shall bruise his heel [*individual* conflict].[4]

---

[1] *Exod.* 20:1-3.
[2] The Greek word *apokalupsis* means uncovering.
[3] *Rev.* 1:1.
[4] *Gen.* 3:15.

- And Jesus answered … 'And I tell you …
  I will build my church, and the gates of hell
  shall not prevail against it.'[1]

The message to look out for? Revelation tells the story of how these two prophetic words will be fulfilled in the final triumph of Jesus.

In this connection, the metaphor of a tapestry or a great painting is particularly helpful. We do not 'read' or interpret books and paintings in the same way. We read books (at least in English!) from left to right. But we 'read' or interpret paintings by looking at the main feature or character in relationship to the supporting facets of the picture. In a sense we are doing two things:

- Exploring the picture from the centre (the main figure, or scene) to the circumference;

- Then exploring the picture as a whole as we take account of how we understand the centrepiece better, as we see it in relation to everything that happens around it.

In this sense Revelation shows us the same picture several times, and as we progress the significance of the picture becomes both clearer and fuller. Each part of the painting draws our eyes in to the central feature or figure, and as we look at them the artist's 'message' becomes clearer to us.

So it is with the Book of Revelation. At the centre is the Lamb who was slain, who is also the Lion King of the tribe of Judah, Jesus himself, incarnate, crucified, raised, ascended, reigning, and coming again in power and majesty.[2]

Like a great painting, it is possible to appreciate Revelation and to feel its impact without being an expert who can explain all the little details. But a little reflection on the structure of the book enables us to see this triumph of Christ in an ever fuller way.

The structure of Revelation is in fact relatively simple. A chief clue is the number seven.

Chapters 1-3—*Seven churches receive letters from Christ.*
Chapters 4-8:5—*Seven seals are opened by the Lamb.*

[1] *Matt.* 16:17-18.
[2] *Rev.* 4:1-5:14.

Chapters 8:6-11:18—*Seven trumpets are blown by the angels.*
Chapters 11:19-14:20—*Seven signs are seen by the apostle.*
Chapters 15:1-16:21—*Seven bowls are poured out on the world.*
Chapters 17:1-19:21—*The total fall of the powers of darkness.*
Chapters 20:1-22:21—*The total triumph of Christ.*

The opening of the seals, the blowing of the trumpets, the signs, and the outpouring of the bowls bring us in a series of intensifying concentric circles right to the edge of the final denouement of history and the end of the cosmic conflict of the ages. As if we were climbing a spiral staircase we walk round and round the same basic themes of Genesis 3:15 and Matthew 16:18 until finally we are shown how it will all end.

First the powers of darkness are defeated. The unholy trinity of the Dragon, the Beast, and the False Prophet along with Babylon the city of man-in-rebellion-against-God are all judged and condemned. Then the Holy Trinity, the Father, the Son, and the Holy Spirit establish the city of God, the New Jerusalem. The Garden Temple of Eden is restored—and more than restored—it is glorified, for God is glorified in it. The order is not so much chronological as theological, biblically logical.

As this vision unfolds before us we surely find ourselves 'lost in wonder, love, and praise'.[1] Christ our Saviour, the Lamb of God sacrificed and slain for our sins, is the resurrected and triumphant King. The Lamb has conquered; Jesus wins. This is the message that put courage into the faint-hearted and nerved the army of God for spiritual warfare in the first century A.D. It has continued to do so ever since.

Thus the story of salvation that began with a threat to the enemy which, nevertheless, contained a promise of deliverance for God's people, comes to its final consummation. The pictures are so vivid a child can be captivated by them and see what they signify. Yet the most learned Bible reader will always be able to see and appreciate fresh aspects of the tapestry. But only the final unfolding of Christ's triumph will fill out the details of how he will bring in his kingdom.

---

[1] From Charles Wesley's hymn 'Love divine, all loves excelling'.

Steps forward

Later we will take up the question of how we apply Scripture to our lives. But for the moment we need to ask: 'What must I learn to do in order to grow in my ability to interpret the Bible and to understand its teaching?'

Most of us learn to do this not so much by reading books (like this one) on how to interpret the Bible. They can tell us either too much, so that we cannot take it all in (we come away feeling we need a college degree in language and grammar before we can understand what we read). Or, on the other hand, a book may tell us so little that we feel we have been left at square one.

What are we to do?

God means us to grow alongside, and with the help of, other Christians.[1]

Of first importance, therefore, is belonging to a church where the Bible is expounded and applied regularly and frequently. Most of us learn how to do something by watching and listening to how others do it. Slowly we learn to go about the task in the same way. To some extent that is also true of Bible study—and is one of the reasons teachers and preachers need to be able to handle the word of God properly.[2]

Bible students can also find group Bible studies helpful. The more capably led they are—by someone who has learned to use Scripture well—the more helpful they will be. But if we are in a church where the Bible is well taught, and where people are applying it to their daily lives, we should give priority to doing Bible study on our own, and in our family. If we are not in such a church, this is all the more important. In either case it would be a wise investment to own some basic helps for Bible study.[3]

We learn to read chiefly *by reading*. So read—and keep on reading—Scripture. The assurance Paul gave Timothy is not limited to him: 'Think over ... for the Lord will give you understanding.'[4] The most important task is to keep reading God's word, letting its truth transform your life. That, as we shall see, is why he has given it to us.

[1] *Eph.* 3:13.
[2] *2 Tim.* 2:15. Hence the warning of *James* 3:1.
[3] See Appendix C, pp. 195-196, for a number of suggested helps for Bible study.
[4] *2 Tim.* 2:7.

8. For Example

ONE of the learning techniques which the rapid advance in communications technology has provided is the action-replay. It allows participants in sporting events to 'talk-through' their thought processes as they scored a goal, holed a putt, served an ace, or hit a home run. The amateur learns by watching and listening.

When we listen to sermons we are not only learning immediate lessons from the passage or text but are often subconsciously developing patterns of reading a passage that we then apply in our own Bible study. We are listening to a 'replay' of the preacher's own Bible study.

This chapter takes the form of a brief Bible study. Having already illustrated some of the ways in which biblical narrative 'works' from the book of Ruth, here we will turn to it again to watch these principles at work in a little more detail. In the limited scope of a single chapter we will inevitably need to be selective. But this may lead us on to a fuller exposition, and then perhaps to study in depth with a detailed commentary. For what the Fathers of the church used to say about the Bible is true: Here a lamb can wade and an elephant can swim.[1]

For starters

What is the best way for us to begin our study? It is always a good thing to try to take the general lie of the land before we become involved in any detail. If we are studying a relatively short book, such as Ruth, we can do this by reading through it quickly, catching the general atmosphere, and noticing the direction in which the book

---

[1] Gregory the Great (540–604) *Moralia* 4.

unfolds. This usually helps us to recognise what each part of the story contributes to the development of the whole narrative.

Covenant promise

Earlier, in chapter 5, we noticed that in reading Old Testament narrative we must always have in mind the way in which the promise of Genesis 3:15 unfolds in terms of God's covenant promise working out through deep conflict to establish his kingdom in Christ.

We should therefore be looking for at least two things:

(1) The connection between what we are reading and the Grand Narrative. In this way we do our Bible study in the light of the principle of the connection between Genesis 3:15 and Luke 24:27, 44-45.

(2) The way in which God's covenant prescriptions and provisions work out in the lives of his people. In this way we also do our Bible study in the light of Paul's teaching that the experiences of God's people in the old covenant were types (*tupoi*) or patterns which provide us with illustrations of how God's covenant provisions and prescriptions, promises and warnings, blessings and cursings actually work out.[1]

In the light of this we can follow the action in the book of Ruth.

Chapter 1: A narrative of a surprising conversion

What is the setting? This will often be our first clue to the rest of the book. The opening words give us the answer: 'In the days when the judges ruled'. The story is set within the period described in the previous book, Judges. The immediately preceding verse in Scripture informs us that it was a period of great instability: 'In those days there was no king in Israel. Everyone did what was right in his own eyes.'[2]

---

[1] *1 Cor.* 10:6. Sometimes these two ways of reading Old Testament narrative are called Redemptive-historical and Exemplary, and set in contrast with each other, as though the former were rooted in Jesus' teaching whereas the latter is a distorted handling of Scripture. Of course if all we see in the narrative is a moral tale ('Be this, not that; do this, don't do that') we are not handling Scripture well. But on the other hand, to fail to see the outworking of God's covenant principles in the narrative is also to miss its meaning. The key issue here is seeing everything through the lens of the activity of the covenant God. When we do so, it is appropriate to read Genesis 18:26 and say not only 'Only Jesus can deliver us from the wrath to come' but also 'Remember Lot's wife!' At least Jesus himself thought so (*Luke* 17:32).

[2] *Judg.* 21:25.

Judges abounds in evidence of the crises which God's people faced, and of how frequently God had to come to their rescue.[1]

We have emphasised that we do not *begin* our reading of Scripture with self-orientated questions. On the other hand we cannot avoid asking, while we are reading, if there are parallels between the period of biblical history about which we are reading and our own.

Obviously some books of Scripture will have special relevance according to the time and place in which we live. Bringing the biblical context to bear on the contemporary context will not be difficult. To some extent this is true of the period of the Judges. Epithets used of our own time seem to be equally applicable to those days, for example distaste for authority and narcissistic individualism.[2]

But it strikes us immediately we begin to read it that the book of Ruth belongs to a different order of history from the book of Judges. The latter paints the story on a national canvas; in the former God is working on a personal, family level which—as the book will only at the end show—has national significance. This gives us another clue to the general message of the book. The God who deals with the nation in Judges is also the God who is deeply concerned about individuals and families. No amount of national need ever distracts God from caring for his own children, however insignificant they may seem to be, even in their own eyes.

These general considerations lead us to examine the rest of the first chapter. What do we find?

The book carries the name of *Ruth*. Yet one of the most obvious features of the opening sections of the narrative is that it is largely about *Naomi*. In order to understand Ruth's life of faith, the writer is saying, we must first look at the life of Naomi. Only then will we see the full significance of the plan of God.

Here is a lesson in both Bible study and in life. God works out his covenant purposes through the interconnectednesses of his people's lives.

What do we discover about Naomi? There are several interesting features, although we will need to read further before we have worked them all out.

[1] *Judg.* 2:16-19.
[2] See Christopher Lasch, *The Culture of Narcissism* (New York: W. W. Norton & Co., 1979).

Naomi is introduced to us in the context of a catalogue of trag-edy and sorrow.[1] Notice the names listed in the opening verses. Old Testament names tend to carry more significance than contemporary western ones. Naomi means *Pleasant*; Elimelech means *My God is King*. Yet Elimelech leads his family away from the land of God's royal blessing, and by the end of the chapter his wife wants to be known as Mara—*Bitter*. Their sons have curious names: Mahlon and Chilion. Perhaps these were originally given to express the spiritual state of the people, since they mean something like *Weakling* and *Pining*.

Here is a strange story indeed. A family leaves the land of God's promise in times of economic crisis. The husband betrays the signifi-cance of his name by failing to trust the covenant Lord in the cov-enant land. The mother carries the burden of two sons with anxiety-producing names. Tragedy follows upon tragedy. The father dies, the sons marry Moabite (therefore pagan) women,[2] and then themselves die untimely deaths.

This is a story about God's covenant. But is it going to be about covenant judgment or covenant blessing? Here, obviously, we are faced with an important question, even if we cannot give an immediate or complete answer to it: What is the ultimate significance of these events for this family?

Question-asking is an important element in Bible study. Questions help us probe the passage we are studying, and disclose its meaning. These may have been Naomi's questions too. Only the unfolding of the plot will provide answers. The same is true in life, where we have to wait for God's providences to unfold further before resolutions become clear. But question-asking, the probing of faith, often leads us to the heart of the matter.

As the story continues Naomi prepares to return to the land of promise.[3] There is surely significance in this. Returning to the land of promise is a theme which often appears in the Old Testament.[4] God

---

[1] *Ruth* 1:1-5.

[2] To feel the full force of this we need to remember that even a tenth-generation Moabite was barred from the assembly of the Lord—*i.e.* Moabites were permanently banned. *Deut.* 23:2.

[3] *Ruth* 1:6.

[4] In one sense it is the story line of the entire Bible: how humanity, barred from the Garden of Eden and exiled to a 'far country' is brought back by grace. It begins,

had given his people the land as their covenant territory. There—and there alone—he promised to bless his people. Now God was blessing his people again.[1] Naomi, a child of God who has been separated from all the ordinary means of grace, now returns to the sphere of promised blessing. Will it be that for her?

Significantly the Hebrew verb that means 'return' in a geographical sense also means 'repent' (*i.e.* return to the Lord) in a spiritual sense. Whether the tragedies of Naomi's life are to be read as a judgment or not, we can now see that God had used them to bring her back to fellowship with himself and his people.

This is a major lesson in the character and strategy of God. It is the kind of point in our Bible study at which we will certainly want to pause to reflect on the Lord's dealings with our own lives, and to ask the appropriate questions: 'Is God dealing with us like this? Have I known his hand on my life in this way? Does this shed light on our own, or someone else's experience?' It certainly teaches us that God is prepared to permit many mysterious things to happen to us, some painful, in order to draw his children back into his arms.

Notice that at the end of the chapter Naomi is, by her own confession, conscious that in her dark night the humbling hand of God has been upon her: 'the Almighty has dealt very bitterly with me'.[2] But she also recognises divine purpose and grace: 'I went away full, and the LORD has brought me back empty.'[3] Empty, but home. There are echoes of this in a much later story about a covenant child who also returned home empty from a 'far country'.[4]

But between Moab and Bethlehem the narrator presses the pause button, and we find that Naomi and the two daughters-in-law who have accompanied her thus far now stand at a significant crossroads both geographically and spiritually. As Naomi returns to the Lord's land, his people and his provision, she is not silent about the costly implications of returning with her to the land and people of God! We can hardly avoid noticing the issue that was at stake, for Naomi

---

as John Milton expressed it, with *Paradise Lost* and concludes with *Paradise Regained*.

[1] *Ruth* 1:6.
[2] *Ruth* 1:20.
[3] *Ruth* 1:21.
[4] The parable of the prodigal son, *Luke* 15:11-31.

underlines it.[1] It is the question of marriage. To continue with Naomi may mean that these young widows will never have the opportunity to find love again and with it the blessing and protection of a husband and family.

This is precisely the question that looms large for many young women when they are faced with the implications of faith in Christ and the cost of discipleship. Might following Christ involve sacrificing the opportunities for marriage and family life? Are they willing to go with Christ's people at such a cost? Can the gospel life be as challenging as that? Indeed it was, and is.

When Naomi hints at this cost, Orpah and Ruth respond quite differently. The price proves to be too much for Orpah and she turns back to Moab. Ruth's response is given in what are probably the best known words in the whole book:

> Do not urge me to leave you or to return from following you. For where you go I will go, and where you lodge I will lodge. Your people shall be my people, and your God my God. Where you die I will die, and there will I be buried. May the LORD do so to me and more also if anything but death parts me from you.[2]

But well known words in the Bible need to be considered with particular care.

Here, for example, the language Ruth uses is much more than the tender expression of personal friendship and loyalty it is often understood to be. In fact her words ought to ring bells in the minds of Bible students. For they clearly (and deliberately) echo God's covenant promises to be the God and Saviour of his people, binding himself to them in a bond of grace and love.[3] Ruth is responding to the covenant God: now he will be her God, and his people will be her people! She is, in essence, taking hold of the promise of the Old Testament gospel, and entrusting her entire life into God's hands.

In essence, this is Ruth's profession of conversion. Despite the presumed closeness of her relationship to her believing mother-in-law in the past, it is only now that God's work in Ruth's life emerges in all its

[1] In *Ruth* 1:11-14.
[2] *Ruth* 1:16-17.
[3] See, *e.g.*, *Exod.* 6:7.

beautiful clarity. It is almost as though a blockage has been removed, so that God's grace can now freely flow to others through Naomi's life and witness. That is a searching thought.

In addition this profession of faith raises the issue of the authenticity of my own. Is this what my faith in Christ means—that I not only take Christ to be mine, but I also take his people? What does this mean for me?

And then there is a question which brings us back directly to the text: 'How will God's providence work out in such a life?'

So Ruth returns with Naomi to Bethlehem.[1] The whole town is stirred. If only that were a more common response! How much we need God to work in profound ways in his children to bring them through to the kind of commitment we see in Ruth and Naomi. Perhaps what our churches most need is the restoration of backsliders and the conversion of outsiders. Then tongues would wag,[2] even inadvertently sharing the gospel, as they did in Bethlehem.

So, as we close the first chapter, we find ourselves humbled under the word of God, praying that he will use his people—including ourselves—to make a similar impact.

But will God leave these two women desolate?

Chapter 2: The Lord will provide

The second chapter begins with a statement which sets the tone for what follows: Boaz is introduced: 'Now Naomi had a relative of her husband's, a worthy man of the clan of Elimelech, whose name was Boaz'.[3]

Ruth's story is set in the context of the ways in which the hand of the Lord came first upon her mother-in-law. Now the author is hinting that God had a further dimension to his plan.

Editorial comments like this in Scripture are intended to be signposts. They help us appreciate the significance of what follows. Here the lesson is clear. God's purposes in our lives are interwoven with his work in the lives of others. He is not threading a single needle, he is weaving an entire tapestry.

[1] *Ruth* 1:19-22.
[2] *Ruth* 1:19.
[3] *Ruth* 2:1.

The first chapter has taught us to keep our eyes open for the providences of God. Sometimes these can be hard to bear. Ruth and Naomi have come home 'empty';[1] they were virtually destitute. Consecration to God is no guarantee that life will be free from hardship and difficulty. Life might well have been more comfortable back in Moab.

Understanding this will save us from adopting a view of life in covenant with God which leaves us disappointed because we later discover it is tough going. It will bring us to a settled knowledge of God and his ways which will sustain us through days of darkness or difficulty. Contentment in God means learning to cope both with having plenty and with being in need.[2] Forewarned is forearmed! We do not read Scripture merely to get a 'spiritual fix' for today, but to learn the will and ways of God for every day.

But learning how to cope with being in need does not mean that believers become passive and inactive.

Ruth went gleaning.[3] Here we may need the help of a concordance, or a Bible dictionary, or the notes of a study Bible to understand the significance of this. God had made provision for the poor by instituting the law of gleaning, commanding his people to leave the 'leftovers' of harvest for the poor to collect.[4]

There is a general lesson for us here. When Ruth and Naomi were in difficulties they found the answer to their needs within the provisions of God's law. How easily we lose sight of the fact that God's law was and still is full of grace.

As we read on we discover that God was providing for their present needs, but also working toward the fulfilment of his ultimate purpose in their lives. That purpose, as the closing verses of the book reveal,

---

[1] *Ruth* 1:21.

[2] See *Phil.* 4:12. Notice that Paul says there is a 'secret' to be learned here. Paul warned churches against the idea prevalent in the 'mystery religions' of antiquity that there were special 'secrets' or 'mysteries' into which they needed special initiation. At the same time he taught that there has been a 'mystery' in the plan of God. But now, through the proclamation of the gospel, it is an 'open secret'—Jesus Christ! See *Eph.* 1:9; 3:4; *Col.* 1:26-27; 2:2-3. The 'secret' of contentment then is to find everything we need in Christ.

[3] *Ruth* 2:2.

[4] See *Exod.* 23:10-11; *Deut.* 24:19. Notice how in the Old Testament 'welfare system' people still had to work in order for their family to eat. Gleaning is not contradicted by Paul's principle in 2 *Thess.* 3:10 that those who do not work do not eat.

had repercussions for the rest of God's saving plan throughout the whole of history. But it begins to unfold because 'as it turned out' ('by chance'!),[1] Ruth found herself gleaning on land that belonged to Boaz.

The story now further unfolds. Boaz helps the women, and provides for their needs.[2]

Boaz is worth a study on its own. He clearly is a mediator of the provision of God. But he is also a man whose character is a reflection of God's.[3]

If we have quickly read through the book to give ourselves a general orientation we already know that he is going to marry Ruth. But we do not yet know something that made him an especially suitable partner for a young widow who had so recently consecrated herself to the Lord and his people. Like Ruth, Boaz was not a 'pure' Jew. He was a descendant of Rahab the harlot, as the New Testament shows.[4] Did his sensitivity to his own family background fit him to take a special interest in, and develop a special affection for this Moabitess? No detail even of our family life is accidental or incidental where God is concerned!

From time to time it is helpful to step back from the immediate action to trace the plan which God has been pursuing. Had these two women not lost their husbands, they would possibly never have returned to Bethlehem. Had they returned full, Ruth might never have evidenced the gracious qualities which she did. Had she never gleaned, the story would not have begun to take the surprising turn it now does. None of this could be anticipated when we read the first lines of the book. God's providences, said a wise man, are like Hebrew words—they can only be read backwards![5] If we have learned that lesson from our study of Ruth chapter 2 we will be able to say with Naomi: 'The LORD ... has not stopped showing his kindness'.[6]

---

[1] *Ruth* 2:3 NIV.

[2] *Ruth* 2:5, 16, 17. See above, pp. 89-90.

[3] Boaz is not, in the technical sense, a 'type' of Christ. But there is an unmistakable Christ-likeness in him: in his dignity of character, his provision for Naomi and Ruth, his patience with their folly, and especially in the way he wins his bride which demonstrates both love and justice. In this sense he illustrates the pattern we saw above in the life of Joseph.

[4] *Matt.* 1:5.

[5] Hebrew is read from right to left, not from left to right as English is.

[6] *Ruth* 2:20.

Chapter 3: 'There's a Divinity that shapes our ends, rough hew them as we will.'[1]

The Bible describes events in a very different environment from ours—geographically, linguistically, intellectually, historically, and culturally. But the human heart is the same. God and his ways with men and women are the same. In addition, the story of the Bible is our story as God's people, the narrative into which our own lives are fitted by the gospel. So the question that arises in all of our Bible study is: 'How do I connect this Bible world to my world, this Grand Narrative to my Personal Narrative? How do I transpose what God did in that world into what God is doing in our world?'

Interpreting and applying God's word for our own times sometimes requires at least a little familiarity with the cultural world of the Bible. We saw this in Ruth chapter 2, in the significance of gleaning. In chapter 3 there are further key cultural elements to understand. One is the idea of the 'kinsman redeemer'.[2] Again, at this point, a Bible dictionary or commentary, or a well cross-referenced or study Bible will help us. They should show us that God placed a premium on family life and gave his people laws to safeguard and strengthen it. This brought great social stability. But that stability depended on people living in accordance with the Maker's instructions by helping family members who were in need.

If, for example, a person was in such debt that the sale of family land became necessary, a relative was expected to raise the purchase price, in order to secure the property within the family. At a later date it could be bought back if circumstances allowed.

We have already had a hint of some family relationship between Boaz and Naomi.[3] Since all Bethlehem knew the story of Naomi and Ruth,[4] we can presume that Boaz also did and was aware of his familial ties to them.

---

[1] The words are Hamlet's, spoken to Horatio, in William Shakespeare's *Hamlet*, Act 5, scene 2. The allusion seems to be to the craft of hedgerow cutting in which one cutter would 'rough hew' to be followed by another who would 'shape the ends' of a roadside hedge.

[2] See *Ruth* 2:20; 3:2; 3:12.

[3] *Ruth* 2:1, 20.

[4] *Ruth* 1:19.

Another institution built into God's law now comes into play: the law of levirate marriage.[1] If a husband died childless, an unmarried brother would marry the widow. Their first son would be counted as the son of the dead man so that he would not be without an heir. This responsibility could devolve on other close relatives. One does not need to read between the lines to recognise that the knowledge that the kindly Boaz was a relative and 'kinsman redeemer' raises Naomi's hopes that the 'accidental' encounter Ruth has had with him might lead to something more significant than food.[2] Indeed the scheming that follows implies it.

Chapter 3 recounts how Naomi capitalises on this new situation. Ruth is to wash and perfume herself, put on her best clothes, and, after the evening festivities, go to the threshing floor where Boaz makes his bed during harvest season, uncover his feet and lie down quietly.

Ruth (naively?) does what her mother-in-law says. When Boaz awakes, Ruth invites him to spread the corner of his garment over her.[3] It does not take much imagination to see that this is the equivalent of a marriage proposal![4]

This is one of the major 'hold your breath' moments in the drama. Boaz, however, demonstrates remarkable composure. He calmly (or was his heart racing?) points out that there is a closer relative to Naomi (and therefore to Ruth) than himself. Should he refuse to marry Ruth, then Boaz will certainly do so.

The tension mounts!

At first sight this chapter appears to be too far removed from the world in which we live to be of practical value today. It seems more in keeping with a Mills and Boon romance than with wise pre-marital guidance for singles! Yet, Naomi's scheme aside, this remains one of the outstanding stories of courtship and marriage in the Old Testament. What can it teach us about this most prized of all human relationships?

---

[1] From the Latin *levir* meaning the brother of a husband. See *Deut.* 25:5-10.
[2] *Ruth* 2:20.
[3] *Ruth* 3:9.
[4] See *Ezek.* 16:8 where the Lord himself is described as doing this in his marriage covenant with Israel.

Despite our reservations about her over-wily scheme, Naomi speaks about marriage in a very significant way—as finding 'rest'[1] or 'a home'.[2] She had used the same expression earlier.[3] It underlines the basic purpose and nature of marriage. God gave it to us as a gift so that a man and a woman might find a home in one another, and experience the welcome and acceptance, stability and purpose, assurance and strength which a home provides.

This is not to say that the Bible's view of a woman's life is that she should always be at home in the kitchen. The 'ideal wife' in the Bible deals in real estate as a part-time venture, and then moves into viticulture! She is a business-woman.[4] But the context for all this is 'home' and 'rest'. Here Scripture teaches us that, whatever the gifts and opportunities a young woman may have, 'home' and 'rest' remain basic needs which God intended marriage to meet. To provide that is the primary responsibility of a husband.

Here, then, is an important diagnostic question a young woman should ask about any man in whom she develops a romantic interest (and *vice versa*): 'Will I find rest and a home in him?' This idea is brought out rather beautifully in the picturesque invitation of Ruth to Boaz to 'spread his wings' (literally) over her. What we have here is a dramatic version of Paul's teaching in Ephesians 5:25-33.

These verses also highlight the emergence of mutual respect and affection between Ruth and Boaz. Here again we are reminded of Ephesians 5:33. Further we should notice Boaz's manly chasteness[5] and his integrity to his fellows,[6] and his kindness to Naomi[7]—his prospective mother-in-law—despite her less-than-subtle and over-adventurous schemes![8] A young woman needs to take careful note of how a man treats her mother! In addition, we can hardly avoid

---

[1] *Ruth* 3:1 ESV.

[2] NIV translation.

[3] *Ruth* 1:9.

[4] See *Prov.* 31:10-31, a passage originally intended *not* for reading at the funeral service of a faithful Christian woman (appropriate although that is) but probably as a vision statement for young women as they set out on married life.

[5] *Ruth* 3:13b-14.

[6] *Ruth* 3:12.

[7] *Ruth* 3:15.

[8] *Ruth* 3:17.

noticing the sense of God that marks his life[1] and his prayerful disposition.[2] Plus there is a beautiful sense of humble gratitude: 'You have
made this last kindness greater than the first in that you have not gone
after young men, whether poor or rich.'[3] Here then are qualities to
desire in a life partner: kindness of spirit that is a reflection of Christ's.

There is a pressing need for us today to be learning these biblical
patterns, qualities, and standards all over again. For all the apparent
culture gap between ourselves and the days of the Judges, God's word
speaks relevantly to the basic issues of marriage, home, and family
life.

A second line of application worth pursuing in this chapter is the
way it speaks more generally to the importance of true character and
integrity. We add nothing to God's purposes by snatching at what we
may most deeply desire, even if it is his plan to give it to us.

Undoubtedly Boaz found his emotions stirred by Ruth.[4] But he
also recognised his responsibilities: loving God with heart, soul,
and strength; and loving his neighbour as himself—in other words,
faithfulness to God, and to his law, and to other men. Boaz stood out
from the crowd. He recognised that the way of blessing must always
be the way of principled obedience to God's word—whatever we gain
or lose in the process. As the teacher in the book of Ecclesiastes noted:
'Better one handful with tranquillity than two handfuls with toil and
chasing after the wind.'[5]

Ruth herself is described as being 'of noble character'.[6] It is worth
our effort to take the time to re-study the pattern of her life and to
discover what qualities led to such spiritual nobility. Is there not a need
for such Christian nobility today? The same characteristic is reflected
in Naomi's comment about Boaz: 'the man will not rest until the matter is settled today'.[7] Here commitment and concern are rolled into
one. Is that present or lacking in our own lives?

[1] *Ruth* 3:13.

[2] *Ruth* 3:14.

[3] *Ruth* 3:10. The Hebrew word used here is enormously significant: *chesed* is frequently used in the Old Testament of the 'covenant love', the 'loyal love' of God
himself. What attracts Boaz is Ruth's godliness.

[4] He says as much in *Ruth* 3:10.

[5] *Eccles.* 4:6 NIV.

[6] *Ruth* 3:11 NIV.

[7] *Ruth* 3:18 NIV.

Our study of Ruth chapter 3 leads us to pray that God will work noble character and true grace into our lives and our relationships, particularly those which we count most important.

Given the language that is used to describe Boaz, it goes without saying that what is emerging in this story points forward to the qualities of the Heavenly Kinsman Redeemer who lovingly and righteously wins his bride the church.

Chapter 4: 'Hast thou not seen how thy heart's wishes have been granted in what He ordaineth?'[1]

So far in our study of Ruth we have been able to trace the character of God and his providential leading of his children through dark experiences. We have seen aspects of the experience of a true disciple in each of the three main characters in the book. Now we discover in chapter 4 that the sad beginning of the story eventually leads to a happy and unexpected ending.

Again much of the interest is centred on Boaz. Did we assume that Ruth is a story with practical relevance for women only? We know better by this stage in the narrative! In chapter 4, several further features of this kinsman-redeemer's life impress us.

Boaz exhibits a strong trust in the goodness of God. We saw hints of this before, but now they come clearly to the surface. There is no doubt that he wants to marry Ruth.[2] But we now see his deepest intentions: to walk in obedience to God, and live according to his word. In God's economy this will lead to his ultimate good and blessings will result.[3] He had no guarantee, however, that these would necessarily coincide with his own natural aspirations. But perhaps he had enough experience of God's dealings with him to say to himself:

> Hast thou not seen
> How thy heart's wishes have been
> *Granted in what He ordaineth?*

Boaz now displays the combination of activity and patience which a desire to be faithful to God and his law produces. He acts. But since

---

[1] From the hymn by Joachim Neander (1650–80), 'Praise to the Lord, the Almighty, the King of creation'.

[2] *Ruth* 3:13.

[3] Boaz is a Romans 8:28 man before Paul!

he acts in accordance with the guidelines which God had set out in his word, and does not overstep them, he is restrained from taking matters into his own hands.

We often fail through impatience. Patience is built into our lives through a commitment to follow God's law, his *torah*, wherever it leads us. Anchored to God's will rather than to our fluctuating desires and emotions, we will not drift. This is a principle that will shed light on the path which we must follow into the future.[1]

The experiences of Ruth and Naomi illustrate Jesus' promise to his followers. No disciple who makes sacrifices in order to serve the Lord is ever ultimately the poorer.[2] Ruth had left home and family for the sake of God and his covenant grace. She would receive *in this world*, home and family, joys and fulfilment, which she would otherwise never have known. Here is truth to fill us with thanksgiving and praise.

Boaz invited the (anonymous) nearer kinsman to discuss matters with him in the presence of the city elders.[3]

The response of the elders to the situation is interesting. Here is a picture of the community of God's people seeking to know his will together. It reminds us of the importance of the corporate care, respect, affection, wisdom, and prayer which should characterise the church family. Particularly impressive is the way in which the prayerful concern of these men is steeped in the thought-forms of Scripture itself.[4] In effect they illustrate the impact we pray for as a result of our own Bible study. They live in a consciousness of God's grace and

---

[1] In this connection it is noteworthy that the Reformers (Luther, Calvin, and others), as well as those who wrote the later catechisms of the church, spent a good deal of time and energy expounding and applying the Ten Commandments—not because they were legalists, but because they realised the remarkable extent to which they provide the Maker's instructions for those who have been created as his image and likeness. They read and applied them as Christians taught by the Lord Jesus (*Matt.* 5:17-48), recognizing that the form in which they were given in Exodus 20 was for God's people (1) as sinners (2) in the period of the Mosaic administration. But in principle all of the commands were now to be understood, applied, and obeyed in the light of Christ's coming and the gift of his Spirit. Thus what the law could never effect in us, because of the weakness of our flesh, is now accomplished in us by the power of the Holy Spirit (*Rom.* 8:3-4).

[2] *Luke* 18:29.

[3] *Ruth* 4:1; cf. *Deut.* 25:5-10.

[4] *Ruth* 4:11-12.

goodness to his children in the past; they trust him as the unchanging faithful Father of his people in the present; they expect him to show the same power and love in the lives of Boaz and Ruth in the future.

What lessons for our life together as believers!

But the punch-line of the whole story is still to come. For the conclusion of the book yields the most remarkable lesson of all.

Boaz marries Ruth. God provides for Naomi and Ruth. But there is more. A son, Obed, is born! Boaz becomes a father, Ruth a happy mother, Naomi a delighted granny! It is a 'happy-ever-after' ending.

But—this is not actually the conclusion. God's plan was far more significant than any of the major characters in this book could ever have imagined. The book of Ruth closes with an apparently mundane recording of a family tree. How dull! Or so we might think. So dull that we could easily miss the point of the whole book. For what a genealogy!

> Peres fathered Hezron,
> Hezron fathered Ram,
> Ram fathered Amminidab,
> Amminidab fathered Nahshon,
> Nahshon fathered Salmon,
> Salmon fathered Boaz,
> Boaz fathered Obed,
> Obed fathered Jesse,
> Jesse fathered *David*.[1]

Here is the book's underlying significance. From the darkness of the experiences of Moab to the throne of David, God was working unerringly to bring his purposes to pass. This is King David's story!

But there is yet more. No doubt the author wanted to underline the remarkable providence of God in the family line of King David. The prayers of the women of Bethlehem for a son who would be 'renowned in all Israel'[2] were answered in a way far beyond their expectations! For the story of Ruth is only the fragment of a larger picture.

Just as the three central characters could have had no idea how the prayers of their friends would be answered through Obed, so the author of the book (who obviously lived in the time of David or

[1] *Ruth* 4:18-22.
[2] *Ruth* 4:14.

afterwards) could have had little idea of the ultimate significance of the genealogy with which he ended his story. But it becomes clear on the first page of the New Testament in the family tree that opens the Gospel of Matthew. This short genealogy eventually leads to the birth of Jesus, the Saviour. It is *his* family tree!

As we set the book within its Old Testament context we see God's providential hand in the emergence of David. When we set it within its whole Bible context the message is breathtaking. This remarkable work of God in bringing a Moabitess to Bethlehem as an ancestor of King David will lead to his greater work in sending his Son from heaven into this family line. So the birth of Ruth's son leads forward to the birth of Jesse's son, David. And his birth points forward to that of another, God's greater Son, conceived not in the womb of a Moabitess, but of a virgin!

Thus the deepest purpose of God for the three characters in the book of Ruth lies far beyond their lifetime. They have been called to be essential links in the chain which joins God's promise to Adam, Abraham and David—and ultimately to the coming of Christ and the kingdom of God. The outworking of God's eternal plan was dependent on the fulfilment of its details in the lives of these apparently insignificant people. Further, their present obedience to his will was the gate through which greater blessing would come not only to Israel but to the whole world.

The lesson is surely obvious. God works in our lives not only for our own time, but for generations yet unborn. Ultimately his purpose in all he accomplishes in his people is related to making Christ known as the Saviour of the world.

When we catch a sense of the immense privilege God has given us by taking us up into his purposes we will, surely, be more willing to yield ourselves entirely to him.

Here, then, we have an illustration of the principle we mentioned earlier. Any passage in Scripture is set within concentric circles of significance.

Here these events—

(1) Had great significance for Naomi, Ruth, and Boaz as they saw what God was doing in each and all of their lives.

(2) But they did not see what the author saw, that these events had a much larger significance beyond their lives.

(3) But not even the author could see that the events had even greater significance. The line God was drawing from Naomi and Ruth to David would be extended to Jesus.

(4) Matthew knew that because he belonged to Christ this was also part of his story. But even he could hardly have imagined what this narrative would lead to and would enable us to say, in Dubai or Denver, in London or Lima: 'Now I know who I am. I have found my roots. They go back to this story and beyond. When God called Ruth he had David in mind, and the coming of Jesus in mind, and my conversion in mind. Now I know who I am in Christ, for this is part of my story too.'

Thus our study in Ruth comes, for the moment at least, to an end. It is time to move on in Scripture to mine for gold in another vein. We know we have not yet learned everything there is to learn from this one short book. But we have learned something from it. No doubt the next time we return to study it God will have yet more light to break out of his word.[1]

---

[1] I have attempted a fuller popular level exposition of Ruth in *Faithful God* (Bryntirion: Evangelical Press of Wales, 2004).

Part Three – Applying the Bible

9. What's the Use?

WHEN you read the Bible, God 'addresses you as sons'.[1] Jesus' sheep hear his voice, recognise it, and follow him.[2] As Martin Luther liked to say, we go to the Bible as the shepherds went to the manger, in order to find Christ. Whenever we read it, we want to be able to say 'Did not our hearts burn within us ... while he opened to us the Scriptures?'[3]

But as the Bible shows us Christ and the Spirit opens our minds to understand and respond to what we read, we are changed. Once, like Paul, there seemed to be a veil covering our hearts. But the Spirit has removed the veil, and the result is life-transforming:

> And we all, with unveiled face, beholding the glory of the Lord, are being transformed into the same image from one degree of glory to another. For this comes from the Lord who is the Spirit.[4]

The Christ we meet through Scripture is 'the same yesterday, today, and forever'.[5] This is not a reference to Christ's eternal nature (although he is, indeed, eternal). It is an affirmation that all he was during his earthly ministry he is still to his people today. As we read the word, and meditate on its truth, and find Christ in its pages, it is the 'same Jesus'[6] who transforms us into his likeness through the ministry of the Spirit.

[1] *Heb.* 12:3.
[2] *John* 10:1-6.
[3] *Luke* 24:32.
[4] *2 Cor.* 3:18.
[5] *Heb.* 13:8.
[6] *Acts* 1:11 NIV.

As we dig more deeply into the teaching of God's word, our lives undergo a transformation because our minds are being renewed through its impact.[1]

This is brought out clearly in the New Testament's greatest statements about the nature and function of the Bible in the life of the Christian:

> As for you, continue in what you have learned and have become convinced of, because you know those from whom you learned it, and how from infancy you have known the holy Scriptures, which are able to make you wise for salvation through faith in Christ Jesus. All Scripture is God-breathed and is useful for teaching, rebuking, correcting and training in righteousness, so that the man of God may be thoroughly equipped for every good work.[2]

This passage is significant for several reasons.

It contains the last recorded words of the apostle Paul. It is safe to assume, therefore, that it expresses his deepest concerns. It is written to Timothy, the young man (now probably in his early thirties) who had come to mean more to Paul than anyone else.[3] He, above all others outside the apostolic band, was to continue Paul's work.[4] Difficulties and stress lie in Timothy's future,[5] outwardly in the paganism around him, inwardly in problems in the church, and in his own struggles in the Christian life. He needs Paul's wisest pastoral counsel. Timothy represents the new era of gospel ministers—all others in the future will be like him in this respect: they will be ministers of God's word, not authors of it. They will no longer get authoritative teaching and guidance by speaking or writing to a person, but by reading, studying, and applying a *Book*.

What Paul said to him was this:

> Believe God's word, because it has come from him and carries his authority. You know that it has pointed you to Christ and taught you the way of salvation. You have seen the effect it has had on the lives of others. You watched your

---

[1] *Rom.* 12:1-2.
[2] *2 Tim.* 3:14-17 NIV.
[3] As Paul indicates in *Phil.* 2:19-22.
[4] *1 Tim.* 1:3.
[5] *2 Tim.* 3:1.

grandmother Lois and your mother Eunice, who taught you its truth when you were a child. You have seen how it has moulded my life and sustained me against the greatest odds. You can trust it to do the same for you as well![1]

John Calvin wrote:

> The Scriptures obtain full authority among believers only when men regard them as having sprung from heaven, as if there the living words of God were heard.[2]

Timothy was convinced that this was so. He had the evidence in others' lives to confirm it. But Paul also emphasised the effect his own study of and obedience to God's word would have on him. So, he added to his statement of the God-breathed character of Scripture an explanation of both its *purpose* and *effect* in the Christian's life.

The purpose of the Bible

Scripture is 'the Spirit's sword',[3] a weapon put into the hand of the Christian. The Spirit uses the Bible to retake what has been enemy occupied territory in our lives, and then to sow the seeds of new fruits in our character. Through it he cuts down offending characteristics in his people and puts to the sword any remaining remnants of opposition to God's kingdom.

Elsewhere we learn that:

> The word of God is living and active. Sharper than any double-edged sword, it penetrates even to dividing soul and spirit, joints and marrow; it judges the thoughts and attitudes of the heart. Nothing in all creation is hidden from God's sight. Everything is uncovered and laid bare before the eyes of him to whom we must give account.[4]

God is the great cardiologist, the supreme heart specialist. He not only makes our hearts the object of his study; he *knows* our hearts. He is a cardiognostician![5] Like a cardiovascular surgeon he does 'open heart surgery.' His word has power to 'divide' (or cut through) 'soul

[1] *2 Tim.* 1:5; 3:14-15.
[2] *Institutes*, I.vii.1.
[3] *Eph.* 6:17.
[4] *Heb.* 4:12-13 NIV.
[5] See *Acts* 1:24; 15:8.

and spirit, joints and marrow'. His surgical skill makes healing possible, and creates the opportunity for a new life to be rebuilt—*from within.*

Paul further describes this work:

> You ... were taught in him, as the truth is in Jesus, to put off your old self which belongs to your former manner of life and is corrupt through deceitful desires, and to be renewed in the spirit of your minds, and to put on the new self, created after the likeness of God in true righteousness and holiness.[1]

How had they been 'taught' this? How had they been 'renewed' in the attitude of their minds? By apostolic doctrine. By the same instruction now handed down to us in the New Testament. Biblical truth, illumining the mind, moving the affections, enlivening the will, leads to the formation of Christian character.

If we return to Paul's words of encouragement to Timothy, we see how this works out in practice. Paul says that Scripture is 'profitable'[2] in four ways:

1. Profitable for teaching

It is sometimes said that Christianity is 'better caught, rather than taught'. True, we do not become Christians merely by being taught about the gospel. But we will never become Christians until we are taught by the Holy Spirit, through the word, and 'learn Christ'.[3] We become followers of Christ through this inward teaching, or 'anointing'.[4] And we will not grow as Christians unless we are fed spiritual nourishment.[5]

---

[1] *Eph.* 4:22-24.

[2] Greek, *ōphelimos,* meaning useful, beneficial, advantageous.

[3] *Eph.* 4:20.

[4] *1 John* 2:20. John says that we do not need anyone to teach us since we have received this anointing. He cannot mean that we have no further need for teaching or teachers, otherwise the letter he was writing would be redundant. Rather he means that, in distinction from Old Testament believers, who were dependent on anointed mediators (prophets, priests, and kings) to teach them what God had revealed, they are now all prophets, priests, and kings because in Christ they have been anointed with the Spirit and have themselves come to know God in Jesus Christ.

[5] *1 Pet.* 2:2.

When we become Christians, we also become disciples, or learners.[1] We place our lives in Christ's hands and he teaches us through his word. We do not immediately, automatically, or intuitively come to know everything there is to learn about being a Christian. There are many things about the gospel that experience on its own cannot teach us. In any case experience is not self-interpreting. We need the word of God to enable us to understand it properly.

Jesus was always *teaching*.[2] People addressed him as 'Teacher', not simply out of respect, but because he taught them about God and man, and did so (unlike their ordinary instructors) 'as one who had authority'.[3]

The Saviour Jesus is also the Teacher Jesus. Yes, he came to be the Priest and King of his people, to sacrifice himself for them and to rule over them; but he also came to be an ever-living Prophet, and to instruct and illumine their minds. That is why the Gospels devote so much space to recording what he said. He preached sermons, he told parables and applied them. We read of him that 'opening his mouth *he taught ...*'.[4]

The same emphasis is found in the evangelism of the early church. The apostles went everywhere teaching and preaching. Paul described his extended ministry in Ephesus in terms of his public and private *teaching*.[5] Again and again in the letters there is this same focus.[6] The people of God need to be taught. Whenever numbers of people are converted the cry always follows, 'Please send us someone who will teach us!'

But, we may ask, why is this teaching so necessary? Why this consistent appeal to the mind and understanding? There are at least three important answers.

---

[1] The English word 'disciple' comes from the Latin *discipulus,* a pupil, student, or learner.

[2] He taught on the mountainside, on the lakeside, in the synagogues, in the villages, in the temple, on the Sabbath, during the week, and while on journeys. There are around a dozen references to Jesus teaching in each of the Synoptic Gospels.

[3] *Matt.* 7:29.

[4] *Matt.* 5:2, literal translation.

[5] *Acts* 20:20. By implication, since he was addressing the elders of the church, he was indicating that their ministry too should be a teaching ministry.

[6] Cf., *e.g., Col.* 1:28; 2:7; 3:16; *2 Thess.* 2:15; *1 Tim.* 4:11; 6:2; *2 Tim.* 2:2.

First, because by nature, our minds are *darkened* and need the light of the gospel to illumine them.[1] When we become Christians, we enter into the light and begin to walk in it.[2] But ordinarily the light of the gospel takes time to penetrate our minds and to dispel all the darkness. As Christians our thinking can still be skewed; our attitudes can remain ill-informed, or distorted. At times, alas, we find ourselves in the position of the Hebrews who needed to be taught the first principles of God's word all over again.[3]

Second, our minds have also been *deceived*. The result is confused, even mistaken thoughts about Christ. We may believe some action to be sinful which, in fact, the Bible regards as legitimate and *vice versa*. We may bind our conscience to a course of action and only at a later stage discover that to do so was inconsistent with our profession of Christ.

This is why the New Testament regularly warns us about the danger of being deceived—whether by riches,[4] by men,[5] by ourselves,[6] by sin,[7] or, ultimately, by Satan.[8]

Deception takes place in the mind. The reason this is so debilitating is that it damages the very instrument we use in order to engage with reality. If the mind is wrongly calibrated our perspective on everything is affected. Jesus captured this idea in an arresting statement: 'If then the light in you is darkness, how great is the darkness.'[9] This is why the warning note is struck again and again: 'Do not be deceived.'[10]

That warning is important. Sin gains ready access to our lives because it appears in a deceptively attractive guise. It was the *pleasures* of sin, not its repulsiveness, on which Moses turned his back.[11] He was able to do so only because he was not deceived about how real these

---

[1] *John* 12:35; *Rom.* 1:21; *Eph.* 4:18; 5:8.
[2] *Eph.* 5:8 ff; *1 John* 1:7.
[3] *Heb.* 5:12.
[4] *Mark* 4:19.
[5] *2 Thess.* 2:3; *Eph.* 5:6; *1 John* 3:17.
[6] *1 Cor.* 3:18; *James* 1:22.
[7] *Rom.* 7:11; *Heb.* 3:13.
[8] *Rev.* 12:9; 20:3, 8, 10.
[9] *Matt.* 6:23.
[10] *Matt.* 24:4; *1 Cor.* 6:9; 15:33; *Eph.* 5:6; *Gal.* 6:7.
[11] *Heb.* 11:25.

pleasures were or how long they would last. He knew that they were 'fleeting'.

John Owen, whose massive writings display a rarely equalled understanding of the psychology of sin, describes its deceiving ability in these quaint, but realistic terms:

> Now sin, when it presseth upon the soul ... will use a thousand wiles to hide from it the terror of the Lord, the end of transgressions, and especially of that peculiar folly which it solicits the mind unto. *Hopes of pardon* shall be used to hide it; and *future repentance* shall hide it; and *present importunity* of lust shall hide it; *occasions and opportunities* shall hide it; *surprisals* shall hide it; *extenuation* of sin shall hide it; *balancing of duties* against it shall hide it; *desperate resolutions* to venture the uttermost for the enjoyment of lust in its pleasures and profits shall hide it. A thousand wiles it hath, which cannot be recounted.[1]

When we are under such pressure (and we are all under it at times), mere knowledge of the Bible will not protect us—we need the God of the Book, not simply the Book about God.[2] But without knowledge of the Book there will be no protection at all. Fail to use the Spirit's sword to unmask the deceitfulness of sin, and the battle to serve Christ will be lost without a blow being struck in our defence. But if we have learned from Scripture to be on our guard, and have grown in discernment through its teaching, we will be able to distinguish between true and false, right and wrong, good and evil, God and Satan. Then it will be possible for us to stand 'in the evil day', and at the end of it to 'stand firm'.[3]

At the beginning of the Christian life standing firm at the end of it may not seem very spectacular. But the longer we live the more we realise that such victory in battle is accomplished only by the ongoing impact of the truth of God on our lives and by his strong grace.

Third, the mind is a *significant key* to the Christian life. 'The secret

---

[1] *The Works of John Owen* (1850-53; repr. Edinburgh: The Banner of Truth Trust, 1965–68), vol. 6, p. 249.

[2] Owen himself neatly distinguished what he called 'the knowledge of the truth' from 'the knowledge of the power of the truth'.

[3] *Eph.* 6:13.

of holy living is in the mind.'[1] If our minds are dull and lifeless, then our Christian lives will reflect that. If our minds are filled with great thoughts about Christ, which then filter into our affections, our lives will show that he stands at their centre.

There is only one ultimate source from which we can learn more about the Lord Jesus and feed our minds on his grace. If we are to have the mind, or attitude of Christ Jesus[2] we need to learn from Scripture what that attitude is.

But how does this work in practice? Paul gives the key to Timothy when he says: 'Think over what I say, for the Lord will give you understanding in everything.'[3] He was speaking about his own apostolic teaching. But his words apply to the whole of Scripture. They are worth writing on a blank page at the front of the Bible we use regularly. Reflection on biblical teaching is our responsibility; insight is the gift which God will give us as we read.

2. Profitable for reproof

Some Christians use the Bible a great deal for reproving. But sadly, they confuse 'reproving' with their own attitude of 'disapproving' of others! That is not what Paul has in mind.

The Bible not only instructs our minds; it touches our consciences. The noun 'reproof' is related to the verb used for the convincing and convicting ministry of the Holy Spirit.[4] He convicts the world of sin, righteousness, and judgment in order to make it conscious of its need for Christ, and of Christ as the answer to its need.

It is a mercy that God reproves us. He does not do this out of malice, for he is not spiteful, but good, kind, and holy. We know too that his word, rightly understood,[5] shows us the truth about ourselves. It is for our good.

The psalmist notes: 'If you, O LORD, should mark iniquities, O Lord, who could stand?' None of us. It is ordinarily only as a last resort that God exposes us publicly. Even when he convicts us of our

[1] John R. W. Stott, *Men Made New* (London: IVP, 1966), p. 50.

[2] *Phil.* 2:5.

[3] *2 Tim.* 2:7.

[4] *John* 16:8-11.

[5] 'Rightly understood' because sometimes Christians misunderstand the teaching of Scripture and do themselves and others harm.

sin and need in the context of the preaching of the word, in his grace he usually works secretly and quietly, although deeply and thoroughly. Under the ministry of his word in the power of his Spirit he reproves us personally and privately. Even the person sitting next to us may have little clue how powerfully the Lord is exposing our sin and showing us our need of the riches of his grace in Christ.

Whenever we read or listen to the teaching of God's word, this question should always be on our mind: 'Is there a word of rebuke for me in this passage of Scripture? Is God touching some sensitive (or desensitised) area of my conscience, in order to restore me to open-hearted fellowship with him?' So Charles Wesley taught the Methodists (and all the followers of the Lord) to pray:

> Whene'er in error's paths we rove,
> The living God through sin forsake,
> Our conscience by Thy Word reprove,
> Convince and bring the wanderers back,
> Deep wounded by Thy Spirit's sword,
> And then by Gilead's balm restored.[1]

3. Profitable for correcting

As a young schoolboy the words 'reprove' and 'correct' seemed to me functional synonyms. Being 'corrected' and being 'rebuked' amounted to the same thing. But in Paul's vocabulary these two words have quite different meanings.

The word 'correction' (*epanorthōsis*) is what students of grammar call *hapax legomenon* ('a once-saider' as my Classics master liked to say). There is no other example of its use in Paul's letters or indeed in the rest of the New Testament.

The word appears however in the Septuagint. There it means repairing something which needs to be mended or rebuilt.[2] Its root (*orthos*) means in a straight line, and so, metaphorically, correct or

[1] From Charles Wesley's hymn, 'Inspirer of the ancient seers'.

[2] In the Septuagint translation of *Ezra* 8:22 (= 1 Esdras 8:52) and 1 Maccabees 14:34 it carries the meaning of putting things right, restoring to their original form. The Greek version of the Hebrew Bible is known as the Septuagint because, traditionally, it was translated from Hebrew into Greek by a team of seventy or seventy-two scholars (six from each of the twelve tribes of Israel).

true. It appears in various English words: an '*ortho*dontist' is a dental specialist who corrects or realigns teeth; an '*ortho*paedic surgeon' sets and restores broken bones or realigns them to correct deformities. Similarly, when we speak of someone's '*ortho*doxy' we mean that the views they hold (*doxa*, an opinion, view) are regular, or correct, well aligned with the truth of the gospel and the lifestyle of the kingdom.

It may be helpful to remember this medical use when we think about Scripture 'correcting' us and making us 'orthodox'. In his correspondence with Timothy the apostle Paul emphasises the importance of doctrine that is 'sound'. He does not mean that our presence leaves a nasty taste in people's mouths! The reverse is the case. When our minds have been illumined and our lives have been transformed by God's truth, then our doctrine will be 'sound' or *health-giving*.[1] We are set on our feet again spiritually.

Perhaps the analogy of the orthodontist helps us grasp the point. The result of his work is a healthy bite; but it usually makes people more attractive as well! The same is true when our lives are 'corrected' by God's word. It gives them bite. But it also puts something attractive into our character.

God's word mends, heals, and restores. It cleanses our emotions and affections. It reshapes our broken lives into a condition of spiritual health and vitality.

That is why it has a fourth effect:

4. Profitable for training in righteousness

We need to train and practise if we are to improve at any activity. So too in the Christian life.[2]

The Spirit of God wants to get us into a healthy spiritual condition. To be precise, he wants to get us into better shape by making us more like Christ. Therefore he trains us in Christ-likeness. All his commands say, in one way or another: be like Jesus! All the Spirit's work in us has this aim in view: to make us like Jesus. The word of God is the gymnasium in which we begin to get into condition to enjoy a full Christian life.

---

[1] *1 Tim.* 1:10; *2 Tim.* 1:13; *Titus* 1:9, 13; 2:1, 2.
[2] Cf. *Heb.* 5:14.

Paul had earlier given a hint of this. While bodily exercise has some value, spiritual exercise has lasting benefits. So, he says, 'train yourself to be godly'.[1] The Greek verb 'train' is recognisable even in English—*gumnazo*, from which we get our word 'gymnasium'. It is as though Paul were saying 'Get into the gymnasium of the Bible and be trained for action'. Bible reading, study, and meditation constitute the training programme in which we most need to invest!

What a tremendous prospect this is. What an incentive to engage in Bible study knowing that it will transform our character and lifestyle!

Think about it this way: we are familiar with the disciplines of sportsmen and musicians who devote so much time and energy in the pursuit of earthly success. Should we not be willing to get into training for a prize which is imperishable?

So the value of God's word is that it teaches, rebukes, corrects, and trains us in the way of life. But what does that accomplish?

The effect

God has given us his word to make us 'normal'. This is really what 'thoroughly equipped' means: being 'normal' as in 'normal like Jesus'. The result is that we become 'competent, equipped for every good work'.[2]

Paul's expression here is derived from the verb for completing a task, finishing a piece of work. A similar verb appears in Mark 1:19. The disciples were mending or 'preparing' (NIV) their nets—cleaning them, repairing tears, and folding them in preparation to be used on the next night. Again the same root is used by Paul when he writes that the ministries of the word which Christ has given to the church all have the aim of preparing God's people for works of service.[3]

God's plan is to restore and equip us for spiritual usefulness. He takes us—broken as we are—and by means of his word (and the various ministries of it in the church), he patiently cleanses, mends, and reshapes our lives, until we are fit, 'thoroughly equipped', 'properly kitted out' for the service of his kingdom.

[1] *1 Tim.* 4:6-8 NIV.
[2] *2 Tim.* 3:17.
[3] *Eph.* 4:12.

God's work takes time. It is long term. Yes, there may be crises along the way. But these simply clear the ground, and remove the blockages. They are the Lord's demolition jobs. But construction work is his ultimate goal. That takes longer.

10. Seed Needs Soil

JESUS told his hearers: 'Take care then how you hear.'[1] On another occasion he warned 'Pay attention to what you hear.'[2] Taken together these sayings underline the importance of the spirit in which we hear God's word.

The preceding chapters have discussed some aspects of *how* we listen. There are ways of studying the Bible which best help us to grasp its message.

But there is another level at which we need to reflect on hearing God's word. It is not merely an intellectual matter. How could it be when the Bible is a Spirit-given book intended to transform our whole lives— mind, affections, will, and dispositions? To hear properly involves having minds that receive and understand the message of Scripture, hearts that respond to it, affections that are cleansed, and wills that are submissive to it and energised by it.

Ours is an instant-access, immediate-gratification world. We search the world-wide-web for information rather than find it in a book. So we rarely learn the context of the raw data we download. It is not accidental that we speak of 'surfing' the web whereas we still speak of 'browsing' in a book. We type in the question and the answer appears, and we are satisfied that we 'know' what we were looking for. But our minds have not been stretched, our understanding has not been increased. The more we gain information in this way the less we really understand.

If this transfers to how we read the Bible the inevitable effect is that we will be Christians who possess Bible knowledge but whose

[1] *Luke* 8:18.
[2] *Mark* 4:24.

understanding remains at the level of spiritual infants. We will treat the Bible as a book of information, not as God's word doing God's work in the hearts and lives of God's people.

So what we need to do is to learn to linger in the Scriptures, chewing, swallowing, and digesting them in order to grow as Christians. Only thus do we allow Scripture to do its own work in our lives. For in the last analysis this is the important thing to understand: it is God's word that does God's work in us.

This is the New Testament's emphasis. Jesus prayed that his disciples would be *sanctified by the truth*. 'Your word is [that] truth.'[1] The word transforms and sanctifies. It works on us and in us. It is sharp—it cuts through to the heart; it convicts and cleanses. It is given to us to replicate in us what it accomplished in the Thessalonians:

> … when you received the word of God, which you heard from us, you accepted it not as the word of men but as it actually is, the word of God, *which is at work in you who believe*.[2]

Since God means his word to be at work in us, our primary responsibility is to have hearts that are receptive as we read it or hear it expounded.

The parable of parables

Jesus told a parable to illustrate this point. In fact it is the key parable—the parable that explains all parables.[3] In its original setting it was a parable about his ministry of the word; but it is perennially applicable.

The parable of the sower (for it is the parable of parables) was so basic that Jesus explained it at length to his disciples—on the presupposition that if they did not understand its meaning they would be incapable of grasping the significance of any of his parables. It was, in essence, his own preaching grid.

Jesus believed that those who heard God's word belonged to one of four general categories each marked by a different heart condition.

[1] *John* 17:17.
[2] *1 Thess.* 2:13 NIV.
[3] *Mark* 4:13.

What is sobering is that of these four categories of 'hearers' only one lastingly welcomed God's word and persevered in it. This, at least was the experience of the Son of Man. That would be a solemn enough thought had Jesus expressed it towards the end of his ministry. By that time people had begun to drift off into the border regions of discipleship and beyond.[1] But our Lord's words, spoken so early in his ministry, clearly predicted that this was the way things would be.

The question with which Christ faces us is: What kind of soil am I when the seed of God's word is sown in my life?

The farmer

The Palestinian farmer went out to sow his crops in a very different context from the modern farmer in the western world. His machinery was his little bag of seed which he scattered on the ground and the oxen and plough he later used for ploughing.[2] As he patiently walked up and down his field he threw the seed down in strips.

The farmer knew a little about practical economics. Not all of his seed would lodge in good soil. Some would fall on the path; some on the shallow soil which lightly covered the limestone beneath—sometimes he could see the limestone jutting out here and there. Some, no doubt, would fall into ground infested by thorns. They would grow together, but it would not be long before the weeds would choke any growth from the good seed.

All this he knew. But he also knew that this apparent waste was part of the burden of being a farmer. Some of his precious seed would never yield the crop he desired. His chief encouragement was that some seed would fall on good soil that would produce a harvest—perhaps even a bumper harvest. That would satisfy him.

As these thoughts passed through his mind he turned to walk over his field once more. He could see the birds swooping down on to the path, picking up the seed which had fallen there a matter of minutes before. Yes, being a farmer was back-breaking work; it could also be heart-breaking.

Within a short time some growth would begin to appear from the seeds which had fallen in the limestone or rocky soil. How different

---

[1] *John* 6:66.
[2] Ploughing *followed* sowing in Jesus' environment.

life would be if the good soil produced as quickly as the limestone soil!

The Roman government would be asking for tax payment soon enough. The farmer's income was a modest sum. He could do his tax returns on his fingers:

> If one seed produced a thirty-fold fruit, and I were able to produce a crop at that rate from a quarter of my seed, what percentage increase would I find in my profits? What would be the increase in my tax levy? If we could do that for a few years in a row then perhaps we would need a new and larger barn!

Then he would return from his daydream. As he walked along the pathway he noticed it had been picked clean of seed by the birds. He knew from experience how short-lived the seed sown on the limestone would be. He had as much as wasted his money on any seed falling into thorn-infested soil. But thank God every year some of the seed fell on good soil. He had managed to survive.

With these thoughts on his mind the farmer turned for home.

Jesus' hearers were familiar with the scene. Perhaps Jesus himself had made ploughs for some of the men in the crowd. He was describing their lifestyle. Like listeners to sermons today, their minds probably went off at tangents as Jesus spoke, picturing their own fields, smiling in response to Jesus' description of a bumper harvest. If only!

The meaning of the parable was acted out before the eyes of Jesus' disciples:

Probably many who heard returned home, telling each other their own stories of failure and success. They largely missed the whole point of the parable.

Others went away, doubtless, wondering exactly what Jesus had been trying to say.

Yet others moved round the crowd as it dispersed, excitedly saying to their friends: 'What an amazing fellow Jesus is, and what an incredible teacher!' But their enthusiasm would be short-lived. They had been swayed by the emotions of the moment. The truth Jesus taught had not sunk down deep into their hearts.

Some others—a smaller group—returned home changed. Even the neighbours noticed. But it lasted only a few months. They found themselves facing trials. Some of the neighbours called them 'Jesus freaks'. Following him got tougher, not easier. It all became too demanding. Soon their enthusiasm began to wane.

But there were some who heard and felt they could never again be the same men and women—and they never were!

Why was this? And why is it *still* this way?

The heart of the matter

Crucial to our reception of God's word is the disposition of our hearts. The all-important question is: Which of the four kinds of soil in our Lord's parable best illustrates me? The pathway? The limestone soil? Perhaps the thorn-ridden soil? Or is my heart good soil for the sower to plant the seed of the word of life?

Pathway hearers

Some hearts are like the pathway. The seed of God's word lies on the firm surface of the well-trodden path. It does not penetrate and take root. The heart is too hard. It is easy for the birds to swoop down and to make off with the seed. So, in the life of the spirit, the devil almost immediately steals the precious seed of the word from our minds. It has no gracious effect—it is not allowed to penetrate to the heart.

Martin Luther enjoyed, and used to quote the proverb 'You cannot stop the birds flying over your head; but you can prevent them from making their nest in your hair!' So what is the problem here?

Jesus puts his finger on two particular things.

1. Ignorance. The reason that the word of God makes little impression on our lives may be that we do not understand it.[1] We have no interest in it.

Some parts of the Bible are difficult to understand. Simon Peter thought that aspects of Paul's teaching were hard to grasp.[2] But Jesus is not speaking about an inability to grasp profound theological ideas. The ignorance he has in view is a basic spiritual inability to grasp the message of the kingdom. This kind of ignorance is caused by a condition of the heart, not by a low IQ[3]

---

[1] See *Matt.* 13:19.

[2] *2 Pet.* 3:16.

[3] This is well expressed in *The Confession of Faith,* I.7: 'All things in Scripture are not alike plain in themselves, nor alike clear unto all: yet those things which are necessary to be known, believed, and observed for salvation, are so clearly propounded,

The parable itself is an illustration. Understanding it does not require a high level of education. But it does require insight into spiritual realities.

Parables are not intelligence tests but heart checks. They reveal heart conditions. As we have seen, they were not intended to be seeker-friendly illustrations but litmus tests. They disclose the presence or absence of spiritual sensitivity. They measure levels of interest in, understanding of, and reactions to how God's kingdom operates. In the case of a 'pathway' hearer Jesus' diagnosis of the problem is sclerosis of the heart (*sklērocardia*),[1] whose chief symptom is an inability to grasp the message of the gospel.

There is a further cause of sclerosis.

2. *Worldliness*. Why is the pathway such an unwelcoming receptacle for the seed? It has been hardened by the traffic of the everyday world which passes over it. The seed lies on the surface and is 'trampled underfoot,' says Jesus.[2]

Our hearts are thoroughfares over which the traffic of the world constantly moves, making them impenetrable. Worldliness is more subtle than we imagine. It has a chameleon-like quality, and can disguise itself against many backgrounds.

But what causes worldliness? Becoming conformed to the norms of this world, rather than to the norms of the gospel, in the way we think, react, and live. We forget or ignore Paul's exhortation not to allow the world to 'squeeze you into its own mould'.[3] The result is that when we come to read or hear Scripture our mindset is out of harmony with it. It belongs to a different world from our own; its message seems strange, unworkable; grace seems threatening; we feel a disconnect. And we assume—erroneously—that our own perspective is the right and safe one.

Our need is to experience the Spirit turning hearts of stone into hearts of flesh.[4]

---

and opened in some place of Scripture or other, that not only the learned, but the unlearned, in a due use of the ordinary means, may attain unto a sufficient understanding of them.'

[1] *Mark* 10:5; 16:14.

[2] *Luke* 8:5.

[3] J. B. Phillips's felicitous rendering of *Rom.* 12:2. *The New Testament in Modern English* (London: Geoffrey Bles, 1960), p. 332.

[4] *Ezek.* 36:26.

Rocky soil hearers

At first glance, the rocky soil might be thought by city-dwellers to represent the hypocritical heart—it promises much (early growth) but in the end produces little. But our Lord's words refer less to hypocrisy and more to superficiality. It is not so much a matter of deliberate deception as it is of shallowness of reception: 'They have no root in themselves.'[1]

Simon Kistemaker well describes the scene:

> At first it appears that the seed sown on rocky places gets an early start. The summer heat, captured in the rock substratum below, is now gradually released in the months of November and December. There is sufficient rainfall, so that the necessary warmth and moisture make early germination possible. These green shoots spring up quickly, and while the rest of the field is still barren, they make quite an impressive show. The trained eye of the farmer sees the difference. He knows that the appearance of the green stalks of grain on the rocky places is deceptive; when the rains have ceased, and the sun in the spring of the year rises with increasing heat, the plants wither. They have no roots that go deep down into the soil to supply the plants with water. The plants shrivel up and die.[2]

'*They have no roots that go deep down into the soil*'. The untrained, inexperienced observer may not notice, but the trained eye of the farmer does. He is not so easily impressed. Long experience has made him wary of such startling results!

The same is true spiritually.

What is the meaning of this? Jesus' interpretation[3] underlines two heart characteristics which sometimes produce startling but short-lived responses to God's word.

1. An inadequate response. Some receive the word 'with joy'. The response is instantaneous, and the sense of happiness is immediate; yet it is inadequate.

---

[1] *Mark* 4:17.
[2] Simon Kistemaker, *The Parables of Jesus*, (Grand Rapids: Baker, 1980), p. 26.
[3] In *Matt.* 13:18-23; *Mark* 4:13-20; *Luke* 8:11-15.

What is wrong with that? Nothing whatsoever—at least nothing necessarily! We would be spiritual Scrooges if we thought otherwise. Christ came to bring light and life, joy and peace, to our lives. The gospel is 'good news of a great joy'.[1] We should rejoice.[2] Jesus told his disciples that bringing fulness of joy was one of the goals of his teaching![3] Joy was a characteristic response to the preaching of the word in the early years of the church's existence.[4]

But why then is the Lord Jesus giving us a cautionary warning? Because immediate, *unaccompanied* joy may be deceptive, and prove to be temporary. '*Unaccompanied*' is the operative word here. If joy and gladness constitute *the whole* of our response to God's word and are accompanied by no other fruit, then something essential is lacking.

Contrast here the experience of the Thessalonians in whom Paul says God's word was 'at work': 'you received the word in much afflic-tion, with the joy of the Holy Spirit'.[5] The genuineness of the joy was well tested by a willingness to experience any suffering that might be involved in receiving it. This was one reason that Paul could be so confident that God had chosen them.[6]

This is not to say that an immediate or a joyful response to the word of God will necessarily prove to be a spurious one. But if that is all there is to it, the new plant is in grave danger.

This is true in the world of nature. We exercise caution about the longevity of any plant that flowers with speed. So much depends on the depth and strength of the roots.

Similarly, says Jesus, when someone responds to the gospel with only joy, then meets persecution or other hardships, the lack of a deep work of grace will begin to show. The hot blast of opposition may cause him to shrivel and die. Here is the paradox: trials and dif-ficulties in the Christian life may kill enthusiasm which is rootless and therefore graceless; but they strengthen the fruit of the Spirit which has developed from strong and lasting roots in the grace of God.

---

[1] *Luke* 2:10.
[2] *Luke* 15:6, 9, 32.
[3] *John* 15:11; 17:13.
[4] *Acts* 8:8; *1 Thess.* 1:6.
[5] *1 Thess.* 1:6.
[6] *1 Thess.* 1:4.

2. *Concentration on the short-term.* How short-sighted we are, and how often our lives revolve around the immediate rather than the long-term! But the working of the word is intended to be long-term. For God characteristically takes his time to work deeply, thoroughly and lastingly in our lives. He is much more interested in roots that go down into our character than he is with the spectacular impressions of short-term enthusiasm.

What does this mean for the way in which we approach God's word?

It means that it produces its best fruit when we are willing to let it work in us over the long haul, through good times and bad. Christian graces, like the best fruits, take time to mature. As Samuel Rutherford famously wrote: 'I see grace groweth best in winter.'[1] This is why there is such an emphasis in the New Testament on being properly rooted.[2]

There is no short cut. There is no substitute for becoming thoroughly acquainted with God's mind and will revealed to us in the Bible and having our responses tested in the cauldron of life. It is through hardships that we enter the kingdom of God.[3] If there is to be lasting fruit, there will be divine pruning.[4]

This serves as a word of warning but also as a word of encouragement. Spiritual maturity is measured not merely by the height to which we seem to have grown but by the difficulties we have overcome to reach that height. It is not expressions of joy but quality that counts. For it is rejoicing *in tribulation* that promises true growth.[5]

This was the confession of the author of Psalm 119:

> Your word is a lamp to my feet
> and a light to my path.
> I have sworn an oath and confirmed it,
> to keep your righteous rules.
> I am severely afflicted;
> give me life, O LORD, according to your word!
> Accept my freewill offerings of praise, O LORD,

[1] Letter 74 written to Lady Culross, *The Letters of Samuel Rutherford*, edited by A. A. Bonar (repr. Edinburgh: The Banner of Truth Trust, 2006), pp. 157-158.
[2] See *John* 15:4-5, 7-8; *Col.* 2:6-7; *Eph.* 3:17-19.
[3] *Acts* 4:22.
[4] *John* 15:2.
[5] *Rom.* 5:3.

and teach me your rules.
I hold my life in my hand continually,
    but I do not forget your law.
The wicked have laid a snare for me,
    but I do not stray from your precepts.
Your testimonies are my heritage forever,
    for they are the joy of my heart.
I incline my heart to perform your statutes
    forever, to the end.[1]

When obedience to the Lord's word becomes more important to us than the experience of joy, then strong roots have begun to develop and lasting fruit may be anticipated. And in addition God gives us joy!

Thorny soil hearers

The first two categories Jesus described involved short-term responses to God's word. In the case of the pathway the rejection was virtually immediate; it was slower in the case of the rocky soil. But the condition represented by the thorny soil can take longer for its true nature to become evident. There appears to be genuine growth.

We would be poor students of human nature and of Scripture if we assumed that there were only two ways to destroy the good seed of God's word. The devil does not disappear from the scene when he has stolen the seed from the 'pathway' hearer or had a hand in the short-lived joy of the rocky soil. He has yet more avenues of approach. For many a person who has remained undefeated by the rigours of trials has crumbled at the hand of ease and plenty.

Spiritual weed-killing is often abandoned when we have plenty. King David is an example of this;[2] King Uzziah another.[3] There is a profound sense in which we need to learn 'the secret of facing plenty'.[4] They had lived with plenty, and sadly had developed a taste for 'other things'.[5] So Jesus warns us against the thorn-infested heart that eventually is drawn away by the cares and interests of this world. He stresses

[1] *Psa.* 119:105-112.
[2] *2 Sam.* 11:1 ff.
[3] *2 Chron.* 26:15-16.
[4] *Phil.* 4:12-13.
[5] *Mark* 4:19.

that the anxieties of *having* and the anxieties of *not having* can equally deal mortal blows.

What has gone wrong? Weeding has been neglected. Thorns and thistle seeds are in the hearts of all of us. Left as they are they will grow. It takes no effort on our part. But the effects are deadening. Given half a chance—which they will be—they will develop and eventually choke what has been accomplished by the word.

If we are inclined to wonder what we must do wrong for this to happen to us, the answer is: *Nothing.* For that is precisely what we will have done wrong: done—nothing. We did not weed out what was alien to Christ. Consequently we pay the penalty: our hearts are diverted and absorbed by a multitude of 'other things',[1] and God's word is neglected.

As Christians we do not want to define ourselves as people who 'don't do' one thing or another. Our goal is to express much more positively what it means to belong to Christ. There is something natural and healthy about this—but not if it leads us to neglect biblical negations. The price we pay to develop the positive graces of the gospel is ridding ourselves of the evils in our hearts. In order to make room for all that Christ has given us, we need to weed out everything which stands against his word and will. Neglect here can only mean trouble later.

The gospel comes to us as sheer, free grace. But Scripture also tells us that in his grace God does not, indeed will not, leave us as he found us. Rather, writes Paul:

> The grace of God has appeared, bringing salvation for all people, *training us to renounce ungodliness and worldly passions, and to live self-controlled, upright, and godly lives in the present age.*[2]

Sin does not need to be planted in us. It is already in us from conception, and will inevitably make its presence felt.[3] The onus is on us to make sure that it receives no opportunity to do so. Indeed

---

[1] *Mark* 4:19.

[2] *Titus* 2:11-12.

[3] This is David's point in *Psa.* 51:5 ('in sin did my mother conceive me'). Rather than excuse himself ('It is my mother's fault!') he is acknowledging that there never was a time when his life was not marred by sin. It is innate.

we must root it out with the help of the Holy Spirit.[1] Christians must learn to say 'No!'[2]

Here, then, are three types of soil: the pathway; the rocky ground; the thorn-infested soil. Each one manifests itself over time. It is against this background that Jesus poses the question: *What kind of soil are you?*

Good soil hearers

How can our hearts become good soil for the word of God? How can we hear in such a way that we receive the word and produce a rich harvest? The rest of the parable makes the essentials clear.

Ploughing is essential. That means we will first of all become deeply conscious of our heart sclerosis, and ask God to deal with it.

Rooting will be needed, in order that we may 'hold fast,' 'keep,' or 'retain' the word.[3] We need to make obedience to God's word a matter of conscience: not treating it in a take-it-or-leave-it fashion, but reading the Bible in his presence, speaking to him about our needs and failures in the light of his truth, and with a desire that his word will lodge deeply in our lives and do its work there.

Weeding will be needed. Constant weeding and heart vigilance are essential if we are to 'bear fruit with patience'.[4] 'Stickability' is itself a great grace. We are called to persevere against all known sin in our lives, trusting that God will keep his promise to use his word to change us, gradually, into the image of his Son Jesus Christ.

'He who has ears to hear, let him hear.'[5]

---

[1] See *Rom.* 8:5-14.

[2] See *Col.* 3:1-17 (especially verses 5-11), perhaps the most comprehensive passage in Scripture on this theme in terms of its doctrinal foundation in union with Christ and its practical application in both mortifying sin and putting on new life in Christ.

[3] *Luke* 8:15.

[4] *Luke* 8:15.

[5] *Luke* 8:8.

11. Speaking Practically

HOW do you actually go about it? That is the question. 'How can I study the Bible so that I will get maximum benefit from it, and find that it really helps me to grow in my spiritual experience and in the knowledge of God?'

In most areas of life it is usually a good thing to compare notes; we learn from others' examples and also from their mistakes. This chapter is simply a comparing of notes. Each of us needs to develop his or her patterns and habits of Bible study. The important thing is to adopt a disciplined plan which is most helpful for you.

Discipline

We have already noticed the first prerequisite to real Bible study. Paul told Timothy that he needed to work hard at it.[1] There must be discipline. Otherwise our study of God's word will be crowded out of our lives, and become an 'extra' rather than a necessity.

Bible study—however we do it—must become a priority. That may not be easy; indeed, at few times in our lives will it be easy. It is not any easier for the housewife than it is for the husband who works from eight to six. It is usually easier to develop disciplines when we are young, and have fewer responsibilities for others. In biblical language we have to live 'making the best use of the time'.[2] We have to purchase

---

[1] *2 Tim.* 2:15.

[2] *Eph.* 5:16. The translation here captures Paul's meaning, but the Authorised (King James) Version expressed a powerful theological motivation by the translation 'redeeming the time'. There is a sense in which even our Bible study is influenced by the cross—we must use time as those who present themselves as living sacrifices to the Lord (*Rom.* 12:1-2).

it by sacrificing some other use to which we might have devoted it. We are not likely to make any real progress until this becomes a settled principle in our thinking.

What does this mean in practice?

We are not bound by the practices of others, although we may learn much from their example. Our task is to get to know, understand, and apply the message of Scripture *however we do it*. It is not necessarily more profitable to study the Bible at 5 am than at 5 pm. There is nothing necessarily spiritual about any hour of the day, early or late. Reading is not necessarily more spiritual than listening to a recorded Bible, even if in general it is for most people the best way to approach Bible study.

Clearly there are obvious advantages in doing our study at a regular hour, where possible. Most of us are creatures of habit and routine. We need structure. What can be done at any time is liable not to be done at all. We are engaged in a long term, not a short term project.

The remarkable young Robert Murray M'Cheyne used to try to set aside his best hours of the day for study. Perhaps we can learn something from that. But some of us are already committed, usually to our daily work, during our best hours.

Can we use time that tends to be given over to nothing very much? Can we make time before work, or could we make time then? Is there time when the dishes have been washed after the evening meal? What about time during the lunch-break? What about that half hour you tend to waste watching television? The programme you did want to see is finished, the next one is only of marginal interest. Yet night after night you watch extra programmes. Why not turn the television off and get out the Bible?

We are all different. Our families and our routines are different. There are no laws which apply to every circumstance—only one necessity: make sure that you give regular time to study God's word.

What about a method?

There are many Bible study aids available today. Many Christians have found The Scripture Union Bible Reading Method helpful, with its notes for various ages and stages providing some comment for each day, and serving as a guide through the whole Bible over a period of several years. *Tabletalk*, the monthly magazine of Ligonier Ministries, provides a wonderful resource for the systematic study of the Bible, and much more. *Search the Scriptures*, published by Inter-Varsity, takes the reader through the entire Bible in a period of three years. For the study of the New Testament the present publisher's *Let's Study* series is specifically designed for personal, family, and group Bible study.

Whatever notes or methods we use, it will be helpful to bear in mind the following:

First, read the entire Bible.

It is possible, without too much strain, to read the entire Bible during the course of one year. You will find such a course of reading printed as Appendix D,[1] which you may find helpful to use. Those who have done so have often been struck by the way the various tributaries of Scripture run together into a massive river of truth and grace. It involves reading only three chapters each day of the year. If it is followed year after year, it will not be long before you are very familiar with the whole of the Bible.

Secondly, read whole books of the Bible in one or two sittings.

There is nothing like reading a Letter or a Gospel in this way—as though you had never read it before and are listening to it as if you were its first recipient. You will find things come home to you by reading in this way which you would never notice by reading only brief sections.

It can also be helpful to read in a different translation from the one you usually use. I still remember the winter Saturday when as a young teenager I spent my pocket money on a paperback edition of J. B. Phillips' new translation-paraphrase of the book of Revelation. I had to walk home from town, having spent all my allowance! But the sense of drama that gripped me as I snuggled in a chair beside an old electric fire and found myself caught up in the drama of Christ's victory remains with me. That afternoon I 'entered' Revelation and felt that I could see it all before my mind's eye; as though I was present, watching the triumph and victory of Christ come to pass. I had

[1] Based on the scheme used by Robert Murray M'Cheyne.

a glimpse, however small, of what that book has meant to so many beleaguered Christians through the ages. I *saw* the message: the Lord God omnipotent reigns!

Such reading experiences do not happen every day. They may be relatively rare. They will often be associated with special occasions, times, or needs in our own lives. But nevertheless we will always benefit from reading in this way—a book at a sitting. It was the way that the New Testament Letters were first read, and it enables us to catch the force of their teaching.

Thirdly, recognise that some books have a foundational significance within the whole message of the Bible and get to know them well.

All the books of the Bible are equally 'inspired'. But clearly some books of the Bible are more fundamental than others. God has given these books in a very definite arrangement. Some of them more clearly present the message of the gospel than others do. Some stress more central themes than others. It therefore makes sense to grapple at greater depth with the message of the central books of Scripture, so that in turn we will have fresh insight into the meaning of all the others.

Because this is true, it will be a profitable long term investment to spend an extended period of weeks or months studying more intensively one of these 'foundational' books. Books such as Genesis, Psalms, Isaiah, John's Gospel, Acts, Romans, Galatians, and Hebrews clearly belong to this category. One day, looking back, strengthened by that investment in earlier days, you will feel that you were a squirrel gathering nuts to supply you in the winter days.

Fourthly, purchase some basic tools for the job.

There are many tools available—almost too many from which to choose. Choose a few.

A reliable translation (*The English Standard Version, The New American Standard Version,* or *The New King James Version,* tend to be the most helpful for study).

A Bible concordance, like Strong's or Young's, which will help you to find your way round the Bible and locate words and passages in it.

A one-volume Bible commentary. Particularly recommended is *The New Bible Commentary 21ˢᵗ Century edition.*

A Bible dictionary, to explain background features that may be unfamiliar to you. Especially valuable is the one volume *New Bible Dictionary* (a companion volume to *The New Bible Commentary*).

Most students find it helpful to take some notes. It is certainly vital to take time to pray about what has been learned from God's word. Prayer makes the soil of the heart fertile for the seed of the word of God. Christians we may be, but we still need the constant help of the Holy Spirit if we are to feel the power of God's word. Pray that he will come to open your eyes, so that you find nuggets of valuable truth, pieces of real, practical wisdom, warning and advice about your life, in the Scriptures you read—and a heart to love, trust, and obey your Lord.[1]

The Bible is a great book. It is the 'God-breathed' book, the 'mouth of God'. That is why Jesus said:

> It is written,
>   'Man shall not live by bread alone,
>   but by every word that comes
>   from the mouth of God.'

---

[1] See Paul's prayers to this effect in *Eph.* 1:15-23; 3:14-21; *Col.* 1:9-14.

Appendices

Appendix A

John Murray on
'The Guidance of the Holy Spirit'[1]

IT is proper to speak of the guidance of the Holy Spirit in the affairs of Christian life and conduct. The question that arises, however, is: How does the Holy Spirit guide and direct the people of God? This is a large and complex question and to deal with it adequately would require extensive and detailed treatment. We may deal with only one aspect of this broad question.

The basic premise upon which we must proceed is that the Word of God in the Scriptures of the Old and New Testaments is the only infallible rule of practice, as it is also the only infallible rule of faith. Complementary to this basic premise is another, namely, that the Word of God is a perfect and sufficient rule of practice. The corollary of this is that we may not look for, depend upon, or demand new revelations of the Spirit. In this respect we are in a different situation from those who lived during the era of revelation and inspiration. During the era, or we should preferably say the eras, of revelation, new revelations of the Spirit were given from time to time in a great variety of situations and for manifold purposes. These revelations were given by direct and supernatural communication to those who were the recipients of them. For that reason they are often called special

[1] From *Collected Writings of John Murray, vol. 1: The Claims of Truth* (Edinburgh: The Banner of Truth Trust, 1976), pp. 186-189.

in order to distinguish them from the revelation which is given in the light of nature and the works of creation and providence. From this consideration, that we must distinguish between the situation in which we are placed and the situation that existed while special revelation was in operation, we derive another premise, namely, that it is contrary to the situation in which God has cast our lot, contrary to the rule under which he has placed us, contrary to the perfection and sufficiency of the Scripture with which he has provided us, and dishonouring to the Holy Spirit, for us to expect or require special revelations to direct us in the affairs of life.

It is possible, however, to admit the validity and necessity of these foregoing premises and yet adopt a position which in reality undermines and defeats their implications. That is to say, we may still fall into the error of thinking that while the Holy Spirit does not provide us with special revelations in the form of words or visions or dreams, yet he may and does provide us with some *direct* feeling or impression or conviction which we are to regard as the Holy Spirit's intimation to us of what his mind and will is in a particular situation. The present writer maintains that this view of the Holy Spirit's guidance amounts, in effect, to the same thing as to believe that the Holy Spirit gives special revelation. And the reason for this conclusion is that we are, in such an event, conceiving of the Holy Spirit as giving us some special and direct communication, be it in the form of feeling, impression, or conviction, a communication or intimation or direction that is not mediated to us through those means which God has ordained for our direction and guidance. In the final analysis this construction or conception of the Holy Spirit's guidance is in the same category as that which holds to direct and special revelation, and that for the reason that it makes little difference whether the intimation is in the form of impression or feeling or conviction or in the form of a verbal communication, if we believe that the experience which we have is a direct and special intimation to us of what the will of God is. The essential point is that we regard the Holy Spirit as giving us guidance by some mode of direct operation and intimation. We are abstracting the operation of the Spirit, in respect of guidance, from the various factors which may properly be regarded as the means through which we are to be guided. Particularly, we abstract the operation of the

Spirit from the infallible and sufficient rule of practice with which he has provided us.

It needs to be stressed in this connection that the Word of God is relevant to every situation in which we are placed, and in one way or another bears upon every detail and circumstance of life. This is just saying, in different words, that we are never in a situation in which we are non-moral or which is for us non-moral. The demands of God's law are all-pervasive, and the revelation God has given to us of his will in the Scriptures applies to us in every situation. It is equally necessary to remember that we must rely upon the Holy Spirit to direct and guide us in the understanding and application of God's will as revealed in Scripture, and we must be constantly conscious of our need of the Holy Spirit to apply the Word effectively to us in each situation. The function of the Holy Spirit in such matters is that of illumination as to what the will of the Lord is, and of imparting to us the willingness and strength to do that will.

It needs also to be recognized that, as we are the subjects of this illumination and are responsive to it, and as the Holy Spirit is operative in us to the doing of God's will, we shall have feelings, impressions, convictions, urges, inhibitions, impulses, burdens, resolutions. Illumination and direction by the Spirit through the Word of God will focus themselves in our consciousness in these ways. We are not automata. And we are finite. We must not think, therefore, that a strong, or overwhelming feeling or impression or conviction, which we may not be able at a particular time to explain to ourselves or others, is necessarily irrational or fanatically mystical. Since we are human and finite and not always able to view all the factors or considerations in their relations to one another, the sum total of these factors and considerations bearing upon a particular situation may focus themselves in our consciousness in what we may describe as a strong feeling or impression. In many cases such a feeling or impression is highly rational and is the only way in which our consciousness, at a particular juncture, can take in or react to a complex manifold of thoroughly proper considerations. In certain instances it may take us a long time to understand the meaning or implications of that impression.

It is here, however, that careful distinction is necessary. The moment we desire or expect or think that a state of our consciousness is the effect of a direct intimation to us of the Holy Spirit's will, or consists in such an intimation and is therefore in the category of special direction from him, then we have given way to the notion of special, direct, detached communication from the Holy Spirit. And this, in respect of its nature, belongs to the same category as belief in special revelation. The only way whereby we can avoid this error is to maintain that the direction and guidance of the Holy Spirit is through the means which he has provided, and that his work is to enable us rightly to interpret and apply the Scripture in the various situations of life, and to enable us to interpret all the factors which enter into each situation in the light of Scripture.

There are two observations to be made in this connection. The first is that the guidance and direction of the Holy Spirit is specific. The guidance which he affords us is in the concrete of our daily lives. The Word of God and the illumination of the Spirit in and through the Word are in the truest sense existential. That is inherent in the belief that the Bible is revelation and that the Holy Spirit constantly seals that revelation in our hearts and minds. The second observation is that our dependence upon an infallible rule and our reliance upon the infallible Spirit do not eliminate all error in judgment or wrong in decision on our part. We are always fallible, imperfect, and sinful. But this doctrine of guidance does eliminate the error of an erroneous criterion. If our criterion or standard of judgment is wrong, then we are deprived of the means whereby our wrong may be corrected. It is one thing to come short in the application of a right rule; it is another to have a wrong rule. It is one thing to limp in the right way; it is another thing to run in the wrong way. In the one case we have a basis for progress; in the other we have not started to make progress.

The notion of guidance by immediate impression, when such an impression is interpreted as the direct intimation of the Holy Spirit to us, distorts our thinking on the question of guidance and stultifies what the apostle prayed for in the case of the believers at Colosse: 'For this cause we also, since the day we heard it, do not cease to pray for you, and to desire that ye might be filled with the knowledge of his will in all wisdom and spiritual understanding; that ye might walk worthy of the Lord unto all pleasing, being fruitful in every good work, and increasing in the knowledge of God' (*Col.* 1:9, 10). In this connection we need to appreciate the implications for godly living of one of the most familiar texts in the New Testament: 'All Scripture is inspired of God and is profitable for doctrine, for reproof, for correction, for the instruction which is in righteousness, that the man of God may be perfect, thoroughly furnished unto every good work' (*2 Tim.* 3:16-17).

Appendix B

John Newton on
'Divine Guidance'[1]

Dear Sir,

It is well for those who are duly sensible of their own weakness and fallibility, and of the difficulties with which they are surrounded in life, that the Lord has promised to guide his people with his eye, and to cause them to hear a word behind them, saying, 'This is the way, walk ye in it,' when they are in danger of turning aside either to the right hand or to the left. For this purpose, he has given us the written word to be a lamp to our feet, and encouraged us to pray for the teaching of his Holy Spirit, that we may rightly understand and apply it.

It is, however, too often seen, that many widely deviate from the path of duty, and commit gross and perplexing mistakes, while they profess a sincere desire to know the will of God, and think they have his warrant and authority. This must certainly be owing to misapplication of the rule by which they judge, since the rule itself is infallible, and the promise sure. The Scripture cannot deceive us, if rightly understood; but it may, if perverted, prove the occasion of confirming us in a mistake. The Holy Spirit cannot mislead those who are under his influence; but we may suppose that we are so, when we are not.

[1] From *Select Letters of John Newton*, (Edinburgh: The Banner of Truth Trust, 2011), pp. 83-89.

It may not be unseasonable to offer a few thoughts upon a subject of great importance to the peace of our minds, and to the honour of our holy profession.

Many have been deceived as to what they ought to do, or in forming a judgment beforehand of events in which they are nearly concerned, by expecting direction in ways which the Lord has not warranted. I shall mention some of the principal of these, for it is not easy to enumerate them all.

Some persons, when two or more things have been in view, and they could not immediately determine which to prefer, have committed their case to the Lord by prayer, and have then proceeded to cast lots: taking it for granted, that, after such a solemn appeal, the turning up of the lot might be safely rested in as an answer from God.

It is true, the Scripture, and indeed right reason, assures us, that the Lord disposes the lot; and there are several cases recorded in the Old Testament, in which lots were used by Divine appointment; but I think neither these, nor the choosing Matthias by lot to the apostleship, are proper precedents for our conduct.

In the division of the lands of Canaan, in the affair of Achan, and in the nomination of Saul to the kingdom, recourse was had to lots by God's express command. The instance of Matthias likewise was singular, such as can never happen again; namely, the choice of an apostle; who would not have been upon a par with the rest, who were chosen immediately by the Lord, unless *He* had been pleased to interpose in some extraordinary way; and all these were before the canon of Scripture was completed, and before the full descent and communication of the Holy Spirit, who was promised to dwell with the church to the end of time.

Under the New Testament dispensation, we are invited to come boldly to the Throne of Grace, to make our requests known to the Lord, and to cast our cares upon him: but we have neither precept nor promise respecting the use of lots; and to have recourse to them without his appointment, seems to be tempting him rather than honouring him, and to savour more of presumption than dependence. The effects likewise of this expedient have often been unhappy and hurtful: a sufficient proof how little it is to be trusted to as a guide of our conduct.

Others, when in doubt, have opened the Bible at a venture, and expected to find something to direct them in the first verse they should cast their eye upon. It is no small discredit to this practice, that the heathens, who knew not the Bible, used some of their favourite books in the same way; and grounded their persuasions of what they ought to do, or of what should befall them, according to the passage they happened to open upon.

Among the Romans, the writings of Virgil were frequently consulted upon these occasions; which gave rise to the well-known expression of the *Sortes Virgilianae*. And indeed Virgil is as well adapted to satisfy inquirers in this way as the Bible itself; for if people will be governed by the occurrence of a single text of Scripture, without regarding the context, or duly comparing it with the general tenor of the word of God, and with their own circumstances, they may commit the greatest extravagances, expect the greatest impossibilities, and contradict the plainest dictates of common sense, while they think they have the word of God on their side.

Can the opening upon 2 Samuel 7:3, when Nathan said unto David, 'Do all that is in thine heart, for the Lord is with thee,' be sufficient to determine the lawfulness or expediency of actions? Or can a glance of the eye upon our Lord's words to the woman of Canaan, Matthew 15:28, 'Be it unto thee even as thou wilt,' amount to a proof, that the present earnest desire of the mind (whatever it may be) shall be surely accomplished? Yet it is certain that matters big with important consequences have been engaged in, and the most sanguine expectations formed, upon no better warrant than dipping (as it is called) upon a text of Scripture.

A sudden strong impression of a text, that seems to have some resemblance to the concern upon the mind, has been accepted by many as an infallible token that they were right, and that things would go just as they would have them: or, on the other hand, if the passage bore a threatening aspect, it has filled them with fears and disquietudes, which they have afterwards found were groundless and unnecessary. These impressions, being more out of their power than the former method, have been more generally regarded and trusted to, but have frequently proved no less delusive.

It is allowed, that such impressions of a precept or a promise as humble, animate, or comfort the soul, by giving it a lively sense of the truth contained in the words, are both profitable and pleasant; and many of the Lord's people have been instructed and supported (especially in a time of trouble) by some seasonable word of grace applied and sealed by his Spirit with power to their hearts. But if impressions or impulses are received as a voice from heaven, directing to such particular actions as could not be proved to be duties without them, a person may be unwarily misled into great evils and gross delusions; and many have been so. There is no doubt but the enemy of our souls, if permitted, can furnish us with Scriptures in abundance in this way, and for these purposes.

Some persons judge of the nature and event of their designs, by the freedom which they find in prayer. They say they commit their ways to God, seek his direction, and are favoured with much enlargement of spirit; and therefore they cannot doubt but what they have in view is acceptable In the Lord's sight. I would not absolutely reject every plea of this kind, yet, without other corroborating evidence, I could not admit it in proof of what it is brought for.

It is not *always* easy to determine when we have spiritual freedom in prayer. Self is deceitful; and when our hearts are much fixed and bent upon a thing, this may put words and earnestness into our mouths. Too often we first secretly determine for ourselves, and then come to ask counsel of God; in such a disposition we are ready to catch at every thing that may seem to favour our darling scheme; and the Lord, for the detection and chastisement of our hypocrisy (for hypocrisy it is, though perhaps hardly perceptible to ourselves), may answer us according to our idols; see Ezekiel 14:3, 4.

Besides, the grace of prayer may be in exercise, when the subject-matter of the prayer may be founded upon a mistake, from the intervention of circumstances which we are unacquainted with. Thus, I may have a friend in a distant country; I hope he *is* alive; I pray for him, and it is my duty so to do. The Lord, by his Spirit, assists his people in what is their present duty. If I am enabled to pray with much liberty for my distant friend, it may be a proof that the Spirit of the Lord is pleased to assist my infirmities, but it is no proof that my friend is certainly alive at the time I am praying for him: and if the next time I pray for him I should find my spirit straitened, I am not to conclude that my friend is dead, and therefore the Lord will not assist me in praying for him any longer.

Once more: A remarkable dream has sometimes been thought as decisive as any of the foregoing methods of knowing the will of God. That many wholesome and seasonable admonitions have been received in dreams, I willingly allow; but, though they may be occasionally noticed, to pay a great attention to dreams, especially to be guided by them, to form our sentiments, conduct, *or* expectations upon them, is superstitious and dangerous. The promises are not made to those who dream, but to those who watch.

Upon the whole, though the Lord may give to some persons, upon some occasions, a hint or encouragement out of the common way; yet expressly to look for and seek his direction in such things as I have mentioned, is unscriptural and ensnaring. I could fill many sheets with a detail of the inconveniences and evils which have followed such a dependence, within the course of my own observation. I have seen some presuming they were doing God service, while acting in contradiction to his express commands. I have known others infatuated to believe a lie, declaring themselves assured, beyond the shadow of a doubt, of things which, after all, never came to pass; and when at length disappointed, Satan has improved the occasion to make them doubt of the plainest and most important truths, and to account their whole former experience a delusion. By these things weak believers have been stumbled, cavils and offences against the Gospel multiplied, and the ways of truth evil spoken of.

But how then may the Lord's guidance be expected? After what has been premised negatively, the question may be answered in a few words. In general, he guides and directs his people, by affording them, in answer to prayer, the light of his Holy Spirit, which enables them to understand and to love the Scriptures. The word of God is not to be used as a lottery; nor is it designed to instruct us by shreds and scraps, which, detached from their proper places, have no determinate import; but it is to furnish us with just principles, right apprehensions, to regulate our judgments and affections, and thereby to influence and direct our conduct.

They who study the Scriptures, in an humble dependence upon Divine teaching, are convinced of their own weakness, are taught to make a true estimate of every thing around them, are gradually formed into a spirit of submission to the will of God, discover the nature and duties of their several situations and relations in life, and the snares and temptations to which they are exposed. The word of God dwells richly in them, is a preservative from error, a light to their feet, and a spring of strength and consolation. By treasuring up the doctrines, precepts, promises, examples, and exhortations of Scripture, in their minds, and daily comparing themselves with the rule by which they walk, they grow into an habitual frame of spiritual wisdom, and acquire a gracious taste, which enables them to judge of right and wrong with a degree of readiness and certainty, as a musical ear judges of sounds. And they are seldom mistaken, because they are influenced by the love of Christ, which rules in their hearts, and a regard to the glory of God; which is the great object they have in view.

In particular cases, the Lord opens and shuts for them, breaks down walls of difficulty which obstruct their path, or hedges up their way with thorns, when they are in danger of going wrong, by the dispensations of his providence. They know that their concernments are in his hands; they are willing to follow whither and when he leads; but are afraid of going before him. Therefore they are not impatient: because they believe, they will not make haste, but wait daily upon him in prayer; especially when they find their hearts most engaged in any purpose or pursuit, they are most jealous of being deceived by appearances, and dare not move farther or faster than they can perceive his light shining upon their paths. I express at least their desire, if not their attainment: thus they would be. And though there are seasons when faith languishes, and self too much prevails, this is their general disposition; and the Lord, whom they serve, does not disappoint their expectations. He leads them by a right way, preserves them from a thousand snares, and satisfies them that he is and will be their guide even unto death.

I am, &c.

JOHN NEWTON

Appendix C

Bibliography for Further Reading

1. Reference Works

New Bible Commentary, 21st Century Edition, eds. G. J. Wenham, J. A. Motyer, D. A. Carson, R. T. France (Nottingham: IVP, 1994).

New Bible Dictionary, 3rd edition, eds., I. H. Marshall, A. R. Millard, J. I. Packer, D. J. Wiseman (Nottingham: IVP, 1996).

2. The Doctrine of Scripture

J. I. Packer, *Fundamentalism and the Word of God* (Grand Rapids: Eerdmans, 1958).

E. J. Young, *Thy Word Is Truth* (Edinburgh: The Banner of Truth Trust, 1957, repr. 2008).

3. Interpreting the Bible

Daniel M. Doriani, *Getting the Message: A Plan for Interpreting and Applying the Bible* (Phillipsburg, NJ: P&R, 1994).

David Murray, *Jesus on Every Page: 10 Simple Ways to Seek and Find Christ in the Old Testament* (Nashville, TN: Thomas Nelson, 2013).

R. C. Sproul, *Knowing Scripture* (Downers Grove: InterVarsity, 2009, 2nd ed.).

4. Bible Surveys

Rodger Crooks, *One Lord, One Plan, One People: A Journey through the Bible from Genesis to Revelation* (Edinburgh: The Banner of Truth Trust, 2011).

J. A. Motyer, *Roots: Let the Old Testament Speak* (Tain: Christian Focus, 2009)

5. Personal Bible Study

J. C. Ryle, *Expository Thoughts on the Gospels*, 7 vols. (Edinburgh: The Banner of Truth Trust, 2012).

Let's Study Series: a series of commentaries on many books of the New Testament written by experienced pastors for the help and encouragement of younger or inexperienced Christians. Published by The Banner of Truth Trust.

Tabletalk, Ligonier Ministries, 421 Ligonier Court, Sanford, FL 32771, www.ligonier.org/tabletalk. Also available for the visually impaired who have access to voice-enabled software. *Tabletalk* magazine is published on a monthly basis and contains Bible study notes for the month as well as articles on various aspects of the Christian faith.

Appendix D

Bible Reading Plan

The following plan for Bible reading will take you through the entire Bible during the course of a year. It requires the reading of three chapters each day. The plan suggests these should be read in the morning, at midday and then in the evening. It may be more suitable for you to find a different schedule, for example: morning, after the evening meal and at bed time.

JANUARY

	Morning	Midday	Evening
1	*Genesis* 1	*Matthew* 1	*Ezra* 1
2	2	2	2
3	3	3	3
4	4	4	4
5	5	5	5
6	6	6	6
7	7	7	7
8	8	8	8
9	9, 10	9	9
10	11	10	10
11	12	11	*Nehemiah* 1
12	13	12	2
13	14	13	3
14	15	14	4
15	16	15	5
16	17	16	6
17	18	17	7
18	19	18	8
19	20	19	9
20	21	20	10
21	22	21	11
22	23	22	12
23	24	23	13
24	25	24	*Esther* 1
25	26	25	2
26	27	26	3
27	28	27	4
28	29	28	5
29	30	*Mark* 1	6
30	31	2	7
31	32	3	8

FEBRUARY

	Morning	Midday	Evening
1	*Genesis* 33	*Mark* 4	*Esther* 9, 10
2	34	5	*Job* 1
3	35, 36	6	2
4	37	7	3
5	38	8	4
6	39	9	5
7	40	10	6
8	41	11	7
9	42	12	8
10	43	13	9
11	44	14	10
12	45	15	11
13	46	16	12
14	47	*Luke* 1 to v. 28	13
15	48	1:39-80	14
16	49	2	15
17	50	3	16, 17
18	*Exodus* 1	4	18
19	2	5	19
20	3	6	20
21	4	7	21
22	5	8	22
23	6	9	23
24	7	10	24
25	8	11	25, 26
26	9	12	27
27	10	13	28
28	11, 12 to v. 21	14	29

MARCH

	Morning	Midday	Evening
1	*Exodus* 12:22-51	*Luke* 15	*Job* 30
2	13	16	31
3	14	17	32
4	15	18	33
5	16	19	34
6	17	20	35
7	18	21	36
8	19	22	37
9	20	23	38
10	21	24	39
11	22	*John* 1	40
12	23	2	41
13	24	3	42
14	25	4	*Proverbs* 1
15	26	5	2
16	27	6	3
17	28	7	4
18	29	8	5
19	30	9	6
20	31	10	7
21	32	11	8
22	33	12	9
23	34	13	10
24	35	14	11
25	36	15	12
26	37	16	13
27	38	17	14
28	39	18	15
29	40	19	16
30	*Leviticus* 1	20	17
31	2, 3	21	18

APRIL

	Morning	Midday	Evening
1	*Leviticus* 4	*Psalms* 1, 2	*Proverbs* 19
2	5	3, 4	20
3	6	5, 6	21
4	7	7, 8	22
5	8	9	23
6	9	10	24
7	10	11, 12	25
8	11, 12	13, 14	26
9	13	15, 16	27
10	14	17	28
11	15	18	29
12	16	19	30
13	17	20, 21	31
14	18	22	*Ecclesiastes* 1
15	19	23, 24	2
16	20	25	3
17	21	26, 27	4
18	22	28, 29	5
19	23	30	6
20	24	31	7
21	25	32	8
22	26	33	9
23	27	34	10
24	*Numbers* 1	35	11
25	2	36	12
26	3	37	*Song of Sol.* 1
27	4	38	2
28	5	39	3
29	6	40, 41	4
30	7	42, 43	5

MAY

	Morning	Midday	Evening
1	*Numbers* 8	*Psalms* 44	*Song of Sol.* 6
2	9	45	7
3	10	46, 47	8
4	11	48	*Isaiah* 1
5	12, 13	49	2
6	14	50	3, 4
7	15	51	5
8	16	52-54	6
9	17, 18	55	7
10	19	56, 57	8, 9 to v. 7
11	20	58, 59	9:8 to 10:4
12	21	60, 61	10:5-34
13	22	62, 63	11, 12
14	23	64, 65	13
15	24	66, 67	14
16	25	68	15
17	26	69	16
18	27	70, 71	17, 18
19	28	72	19, 20
20	29	73	21
21	30	74	22
22	31	75, 76	23
23	32	77	24
24	33	78 to v. 37	25
25	34	78:38-72	26
26	35	79	27
27	36	80	28
28	*Deuteronomy* 1	81, 82	29
29	2	83, 84	30
30	3	85	31
31	4	86, 87	32

JUNE

	Morning	Midday	Evening
1	Deuteronomy 5	Psalms 88	Isaiah 33
2	6	89	34
3	7	90	35
4	8	91	36
5	9	92, 93	37
6	10	94	38
7	11	95, 96	39
8	12	97, 98	40
9	13, 14	99-101	41
10	15	102	42
11	16	103	43
12	17	104	44
13	18	105	45
14	19	106	46
15	20	107	47
16	21	108, 109	48
17	22	110, 111	49
18	23	112, 113	50
19	24	114, 115	51
20	25	116	52
21	26	117, 118	53
22	27, 28 to v. 19	119 to v. 24	54
23	28:20-68	119:25-48	55
24	29	119:49-72	56
25	30	119:73-96	57
26	31	119:97-120	58
27	32	119:121-144	59
28	33, 34	119:145-176	60
29	Joshua 1	120-122	61
30	2	123-125	62

JULY

	Morning	Midday	Evening
1	*Joshua* 3	*Psalms* 126-128	*Isaiah* 63
2	4	129-131	64
3	5, 6 to v. 5	132-134	65
4	6:6-27	135, 136	66
5	7	137, 138	*Jeremiah* 1
6	8	139	2
7	9	140, 141	3
8	10	142, 143	4
9	11	144	5
10	12, 13	145	6
11	14, 15	146, 147	7
12	16, 17	148	8
13	18, 19	149, 150	9
14	20, 21	*Acts* 1	10
15	22	2	11
16	23	3	12
17	24	4	13
18	*Judges* 1	5	14
19	2	6	15
20	3	7	16
21	4	8	17
22	5	9	18
23	6	10	19
24	7	11	20
25	8	12	21
26	9	13	22
27	10, 11 to v. 11	14	23
28	11:12-40	15	24
29	12	16	25
30	13	17	26
31	14	18	27

AUGUST

	Morning	Midday	Evening
1	*Judges* 15	*Acts* 19	*Jeremiah* 28
2	16	20	29
3	17	21	30, 31
4	18	22	32
5	19	23	33
6	20	24	34
7	21	25	35
8	*Ruth* 1	26	36, 45
9	2	27	37
10	3	28	38
11	4	*Romans* 1	39
12	*1 Samuel* 1	2	40
13	2	3	41
14	3, 4	4	42
15	5, 6	5	43
16	7, 8	6	44
17	9	7	46
18	10	8	47
19	11	9	48
20	12	10	49
21	13	11	50
22	14	12	51
23	15	13	52
24	16	14	*Lamentations* 1
25	17	15	2
26	18	16	3
27	19	*1 Corinthians* 1	4
28	20	2	5
29	21, 22	3	*Ezekiel* 1
30	23	4	2
31	24	5	3

SEPTEMBER

	Morning	Midday	Evening
1	*1 Samuel* 25	*1 Corinthians* 6	*Ezekiel* 4
2	26	7	5
3	27	8	6
4	28	9	7
5	29, 30	10	8
6	31	11	9
7	*2 Samuel* 1	12	10
8	2	13	11
9	3	14	12
10	4, 5	15	13
11	6	16	14
12	7	*2 Corinthians* 1	15
13	8, 9	2	16
14	10	3	17
15	11	4	18
16	12	5	19
17	13	6	20
18	14	7	21
19	15	8	22
20	16	9	23
21	17	10	24
22	18	11	25
23	19	12	26
24	20	13	27
25	21	*Galatians* 1	28
26	22	2	29
27	23	3	30
28	24	4	31
29	*1 Kings* 1	5	32
30	2	6	33

OCTOBER

	Morning	Midday	Evening
1	*1 Kings* 3	*Ephesians* 1	*Ezekiel* 34
2	4, 5	2	35
3	6	3	36
4	7	4	37
5	8	5	38
6	9	6	39
7	10	*Philippians* 1	40
8	11	2	41
9	12	3	42
10	13	4	43
11	14	*Colossians* 1	44
12	15	2	45
13	16	3	46
14	17	4	47
15	18	*1 Thessalonians* 1	48
16	19	2	*Daniel* 1
17	20	3	2
18	21	4	3
19	22	5	4
20	*2 Kings* 1	*2 Thessalonians* 1	5
21	2	2	6
22	3	3	7
23	4	*1 Timothy* 1	8
24	5	2	9
25	6	3	10
26	7	4	11
27	8	5	12
28	9	6	*Hosea* 1
29	10	*2 Timothy* 1	2
30	11, 12	2	3, 4
31	13	3	5, 6

NOVEMBER

	Morning	Midday	Evening
1	2 Kings 14	2 Timothy 4	Hosea 7
2	15	Titus 1	8
3	16	2	9
4	17	3	10
5	18	Philemon 1	11
6	19	Hebrews 1	12
7	20	2	13
8	21	3	14
9	22	4	Joel 1
10	23	5	2
11	24	6	3
12	25	7	Amos 1
13	1 Chronicles 1, 2	8	2
14	3, 4	9	3
15	5, 6	10	4
16	7, 8	11	5
17	9, 10	12	6
18	11, 12	13	7
19	13, 14	James 1	8
20	15	2	9
21	16	3	Obadiah 1
22	17	4	Jonah 1
23	18	5	2
24	19, 20	1 Peter 1	3
25	21	2	4
26	22	3	Micah 1
27	23	4	2
28	24, 25	5	3
29	26, 27	2 Peter 1	4
30	28	2	5

DECEMBER

	Morning	Midday	Evening
1	*1 Chronicles* 29	*2 Peter* 3	*Micah* 6
2	*2 Chronicles* 1	*1 John* 1	7
3	2	2	*Nahum* 1
4	3, 4	3	2
5	5, 6 to v. 11	4	3
6	6:12-42	5	*Habakkuk* 1
7	7	*2 John* 1	2
8	8	*3 John* 1	3
9	9	*Jude* 1	*Zephaniah* 1
10	10	*Revelation* 1	2
11	11, 12	2	3
12	13	3	*Haggai* 1
13	14, 15	4	2
14	16	5	*Zechariah* 1
15	17	6	2
16	18	7	3
17	19, 20	8	4
18	21	9	5
19	22, 23	10	6
20	24	11	7
21	25	12	8
22	26	13	9
23	27, 28	14	10
24	29	15	11
25	30	16	12, 13 to v. 1
26	31	17	13:2-9
27	32	18	14
28	33	19	*Malachi* 1
29	34	20	2
30	35	21	3
31	36	22	4

About the Publisher

The Banner of Truth Trust originated in 1957 in London. The founders believed that much of the best literature of historic Christianity had been allowed to fall into oblivion and that, under God, its recovery could well lead not only to a strengthening of the church, but to true revival.

Inter-denominational in vision, this publishing work is now international, and our lists include a number of contemporary authors along with classics from the past. The translation of these books into many languages is encouraged.

A monthly magazine, *The Banner of Truth*, is also published and further information will be gladly supplied by either of the offices below or from our website.

THE BANNER OF TRUTH TRUST

3 Murrayfield Road
Edinburgh, EH12 6EL
UK

PO Box 621, Carlisle
Pennsylvania, 17013
USA

www.banneroftruth.co.uk

This book is provided by

TRUTHFORLIFE®
THE BIBLE-TEACHING MINISTRY OF **ALISTAIR BEGG**

At Truth For Life, our mission is to teach the Bible with clarity and relevance so that unbelievers will be converted, believers will be established, and local churches will be strengthened.

Since 1995, Truth For Life has aired a Bible-teaching broadcast on the radio, which is now distributed on over 1,600 radio outlets each day, and freely on podcast and on the Truth For Life mobile app. Additionally, a large content archive of full-length Bible-teaching sermons is available for free download at www.truthforlife.org.

Truth For Life also makes full-length Bible-teaching available on CD and DVD. These materials, and also books authored by Alistair Begg, are made available at cost, with no markup, so that price is not a barrier to those seeking a deeper understanding of God's Word.

The ministry connects with listeners at live listener and pastor events and conferences across the U.S. and Canada in cities where the radio program is heard.

Contact Truth For Life

In the U.S.:
PO Box 398000, Cleveland, OH 44139 1.888.588.7884
www.truthforlife.org   letters@truthforlife.org

In Canada:
P.O. Box 19008, Delta, BC V4L 2P8   1.877.518.7884
www.truthforlife.ca   letters@truthforlife.ca

And also at:
www.facebook.com/truthforlife   www.twitter.com/truthforlife